Built in USA

1932-1944

Edited by Elizabeth Mock
Foreword by Philip L. Goodwin

Post-war Architecture

Edited by Henry-Russell Hitchcock and Arthur Drexler

The Museum of Modern Art, New York
Reprint Edition, 1968
Published for The Museum of Modern Art by Arno Press

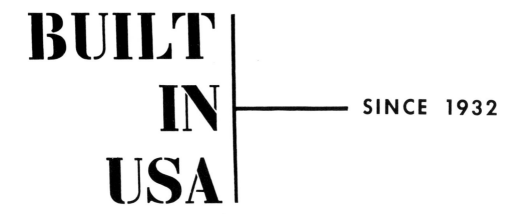

BUILT IN USA — SINCE 1932

EDITED BY ELIZABETH MOCK
FOREWORD BY PHILIP L. GOODWIN

THE MUSEUM OF MODERN ART, NEW YORK

CONTENTS

ACKNOWLEDGMENTS

The Department of Architecture wishes to express its gratitude to the *Architectural Forum, Pencil Points* and the *Architectural Record,* for the many plans and drawings which were reproduced from their pages; Carl Feiss, for photographs of the Red Rocks Amphitheatre; Charles Sheeler, for his photograph of the Bucks County Barn; the Chicago Park District, for photographs of the pedestrian passerelle; the Farm Security Administration, for photographs of the FSA communities; the National Housing Agency, for photographs of Valencia Gardens and Windsor Locks housing; the Manhattan Department of Borough Works, for photographs of the Asphalt Plant; the Tennessee Valley Authority, for photographs of Norris Dam and the Watts Bar Steam Plant; the M.I.T. *Technology Review,* for photographs of the M.I.T. swimming pool; and the many private photographers whose work appears in this book, and who are listed below.

Thanks are also due to Alfred H. Barr, Jr., for his criticism of the text; to Philip Johnson, for his help with the design of the exhibition; and to those staff members, Anne Tredick and Frances Pernas, for their valuable assistance.

E.B.M.

Names and Addresses of Photographers

Rollin Bailey, care of David W. Bailey, Lehman Hall, Cambridge, Mass.; Esther Born, 730 Montgomery St., San Francisco, Cal.; Walter Boychuk, 1015 S. W. Broadway, Portland, Ore.; Cushing-Gellatly, 603 Boylston Street, Boston, Mass.; Robert Damora, 38 East 61st St., New York; Fred Dapprich, 1007 N. Coronado Terrace, Los Angeles, Cal.; Paul Davis, Mass. Ave. at Newbury St., Boston, Mass.; Leonard Delano, 3734 N. E. Chico St., Portland, Ore.; R. T. Dooner, 1724 Chestnut St., Philadelphia, Pa.; Eliot Elisofon, 41 West 54th St., New York; Ernest Funk, c/o John Funk, 33 Ardmore Rd., Berkeley, Cal.; Gottscho-Schleisner, 150–35 86th Ave., Jamaica, N. Y.; P. E. Guerrero, 37 N. Mesa Dr., Mesa, Ariz.; Arthur C. Haskell, 21 Cedar St., Marblehead, Mass.; Hedrich-Blessing Studio, 450 E. Ohio St., Chicago, Ill.; Leavenworth's, 1315 W. Michigan Ave., Lansing, Mich.; F. S. Lincoln, 114 E. 32nd St., New York; Margaret Lowe, 676 South Rampart, Los Angeles, Cal.; Luckhaus Studio, 2716 W. 7th St., Los Angeles, Cal.; Rodney McCay Morgan, 527 E. 72nd St., New York; Photo-Art Commercial Studios 420 S. W. Washington St., Portland, Ore.; Ben Schnall, c/o *Yank* Magazine, 205 E. 42nd St., New York; Julius Shulman, 523 N. Boylston St., Los Angeles, Cal.; R. W. St. Clair, 92 Henry St., Cambridge, Mass.; Ezra Stoller, 3115 Sedgewick Ave., New York; Roger Sturtevant, 730 Montgomery St., San Francisco, Cal.; Thomas Airviews, 38–03 207th St., Bayside, N. Y.; William Ward, 425 Fifth Ave., New York; Western Airphoto Co.

Photograph Credits

pp.26–7, Hedrich-Blessing; pp.28–9, Leavenworth's; p.30 (top and lower left) Sturtevant, (lower right) Funk; pp.31–33, Sturtevant; pp.34–5, Dapprich; pp.36–7, Stoller; p.38, (top) Haskell, (bottom) Bailey; p.39, (top) Haskell, (bottom) Bailey; pp.40–1, (top) Boychuk, (lower left and right) Photo-Art Commercial Studios; pp.42–3, Stoller; pp.44–5, Schnall; p.46, Cushing-Gellatly; p.47, Stoller; pp.48–9, Damora; pp.50–1, Gottscho-Schleisner; pp.52–3, Shulman; p.54, (left) St. Clair, (right) Stoller; p.55, Stoller; pp.56–7, Lowe; p.58, NHA; p.59, Sturtevant; pp.60–63, FSA; p.64, (first and third) Davis, (second and fourth) NHA; pp.66–7, Gottscho-Schleisner; pp.68–71, Shulman; pp.72–3, Luckhaus Studio; pp.74–5, Hedrich-Blessing; pp.76–7, Born; pp.78–9, Sturtevant; pp.80–1, Hedrich-Blessing; p.82, Haskell; p.83, (top) Haskell, (bottom) *Technology Review*; pp.84–6, Guerrero; p.87, courtesy Carl Feiss; p.88, Damora; p.89, (top) Elisofon, (bottom) Damora; pp.90–1, Sturtevant; pp.92–97, Hedrich-Blessing; p.99, (top) Ward, (lower left and right) Manhattan Dept. of Borough Works; p.100, Dooner; p.101, Schnall; p.102, Lincoln; p.103, Thomas Airviews; pp.104–5, Sturtevant; pp.106–7, Delano; pp.108–9, Shulman; p.110, Western Airphoto Co.; pp.111–13, TVA; p.114, (upper) Morgan, (lower) Chicago Park District; p.115, Morgan.

The path of the Department of Architecture in the Museum of Modern Art has not been too easy. Architecture is not well understood by the great public and even if examples are carefully documented with photographs, clear drawings and good models, it still remains difficult and slow to digest as compared with the excitement of contemplating glowing colors, exotic shapes and tantalizing ideas in modern painting.

The Department had been proposed by Alfred H. Barr, Jr., as part of the original plan for the Museum, but painting and sculpture absorbed the entire energies of the small staff for the first two years. In 1931 a couple of young men in their middle twenties, full of enthusiasm for the subject, Philip Johnson and Henry-Russell Hitchcock, Jr., were fortunately ready to give time, thought and travel to the initial steps that were projected. These were a library of architectural photographs and a guide to existing modern European building. In the spring of 1932 they prepared an exhibition of foreign and native examples of true contemporary design called an *International Exhibition of Modern Architecture,* held in the Museum's first quarters in the Heckscher Building, New York.

This architecture was so new and surprising that hostile and ill-informed critics and architects still frequently assert that the Museum is trying to impose a foreign style on the United States. Such was not the Museum's intention in the first place, nor has it been the Museum's program since. First to proclaim the new European architecture here and constantly interested in its more recent developments, the Museum has also been first to show the growth of an authentic modern American style, its relationship to the American background and its debt to, as well as its reaction from, the "International Style."

On page 124 is a complete list of architectural exhibitions from 1932 to date including the circulating shows, which sometimes derived from the large New York displays and sometimes were entirely independent of them. From short circuits to those of nation-wide scope, the Museum has widened its range as far as Paris, Cairo and Rio de Janeiro; London and Stockholm; Mexico City and Toronto.

The Museum has always pointed out the desperate need for city planning, but the lack of visual material in this field has been an obstacle to any major show. The small new exhibition of neighborhood planning principles, *Look at Your Neighborhood,* prepared in two hundred copies for sale to civic groups, has met with so much popular enthusiasm that it may become the first of a series of such enterprises.

In addition to catalogs issued with these exhibitions, a list of which is appended on page 127, several independent publications were printed, notably *The Architecture of H. H. Richardson and His Times* by H.-R. Hitchcock (1936); a *Guide to Modern Architecture in the Northeast States* by John McAndrew (1940); *What is Modern Architecture?* (1942); and *Brazil Builds* (1943). It is a curious fact that although London, Copenhagen and Stockholm all have had cheap illustrated guides to modern buildings, the similar guide to the Northeast States priced at twenty-five cents was sold here with extreme difficulty. The reason for this was that it was too cheap. In the United States, newstands will stock a ten cent magazine that sells in thousands but not one that might sell in hundreds. More expensive bookshops have not enough room for a little book on which they make only a trifle. It is possible that, included in a library like Penguin or Pocket Books, such a reference book covering all parts of this country might attain the circulation it should have.

After exhibitions and publications there are two other activities of the Department that need extension. Thus far only two films have been attempted, and these on a very modest scale; they should be followed with others. The Department has also arranged for lectures from time to time. In addition to arranging a tour for Le Corbusier in 1935, the Department has collaborated with other Museum departments in arranging lectures by Alvar Aalto and Walter Gropius, and in the early summer of 1944 a series of lectures and a forum on problems of planning. John McAndrew, as Curator of Architecture, lectured in fifteen states.

The Museum has long been convinced that architects for government buildings must be chosen by the democratic method of open, anonymous competition if American official architecture is ever to get out of its long-accustomed rut. A competition for a National Gallery of Art might have resulted in something more lively than the costly mummy which now faces the Mall. Encouragement of architectural competitions through exhibitions of prize-winning plans has been an important part of the Department's activity, and in 1938 the Department, with the *Architectural Forum,* conducted a large competition for a new art center at Wheaton College. This was perhaps the first time that an American college was willing or, indeed, eager to have a building of non-traditional design.

Finally, the Department of Architecture acts as a clearing-house for information on modern architecture here and abroad, and is frequently consulted by people about to build. Its research file of more than five thousand photographs is in constant use by writers, magazine editors, students and interested laymen. The unrivalled European collection has been the major source of illustrations for all manner of architectural publications.

1944 brings us to the twelfth year of the Department of Architecture, and the fifteenth anniversary of the Museum. At last it is presenting an exhibition of recent good building in the United States, to be repeated every other year if conditions permit. This exhibition covers the period since 1932, which was the Museum's first, and until now most recent, attempt to select outstanding examples of contemporary American architecture. If and when this review is repeated in the future, as Alfred Barr and Dean Joseph Hudnut, of Harvard, have so long urged, let us hope that it will include many more types of buildings.

The Executive Committee for the exhibition, composed of Elizabeth Mock, Alfred Barr and myself, felt from the beginning that, since personal inspection of possible inclusions would in most cases be out of the question, we should seek the

THE MANNER OF
SELECTION

6

advice of as many responsible people as possible, all over the country. With this in mind a special Advisory Committee was formed which would supplement the regular Architecture Committee, many of whom were in the armed services. In addition, letters and questionnaires were sent to more than three hundred architects and interested laymen in all parts of the United States. Members of the Architecture and Advisory Committees were urged to come in to the Museum to discuss the new material which was received.

From the beginning it was stipulated that selections would be limited to executed work, even though this meant the omission of important projects. The Committee's first decision was to limit the representation of any one architect to three examples. The second was to exclude temporary exposition pavilions, whether designed by foreign architects or by Americans. It was also decided that the Saarinens' winning project for the Smithsonian competition should be illustrated in the book even though it was not eligible for inclusion among the actual selections. And finally, it was agreed that we were not in a position to treat landscaping as a separate category, although it would naturally assume an important place in the consideration of individual buildings.

Happily the Committee made thirty-six selections without any violent differences of opinion. At the conclusion of the meeting the Executive Committee was given the power to expand the list to fifty if they so chose. Eleven additions were later made by the Executive Committee, all buildings in which some of the larger Committee had expressed strong interest, and the result is the forty-seven buildings shown on pages 26 to 116 of this book and featured in the architectural section of the Museum's Fifteenth Anniversary Exhibition, *Art in Progress,* in the summer of 1944.

The wealth of good building in the fourteen years since the original *Modern Architecture* show made the process of selection extremely difficult. A few buildings were, it is true, chosen for special reasons, but the great majority was selected on the basis of total design. The list by no means covers *all* the excellent modern buildings of the period, nor, perhaps unjustly, does it represent many architects who have turned out consistently good work, but have not yet happened to produce any one building which the Committee could agree upon as a distinguished architectural achievement. Some of these omissions will be preferred by many people to this or that building which is included in this book. And many critics will object to the relatively small number of categories which are represented. Where are the attractive open-front shops developed in the last decade? Why are there no apartment houses, tourist camps, or filling-stations—all typical of our time?

The war has driven back into the railroad stations millions who doubtless expected never to use one again; interesting small examples do exist but they are very few indeed. Transportation's newest feature and greatest architectural prospect, the airport, has nothing better to offer so far than the Washington one unless it is in the military sphere. Railroad stations began a hundred years ago and reached their high point in the iron sheds of the late nineteenth century—

about half way between rise and decline. So it may be with the airport which has not yet got into its second quarter, although one would expect it to reach a peak with greater speed than its predecessor. The American public frequents the movie houses now with more devotion than the faithful used to fill their churches. With the usual high opinion of the amusement business men in the United States for their public, they began to feed them with debased "styles" which have been succeeded by a very few small movie houses with many good points. The Committee is conscious of the progressive work that has been done in these fields, yet feels that over-insistence on categorical or geographical representations would have weakened the results in terms of standards.

It is perhaps in the field of domestic architecture that our list is strongest; and that is only natural, for that is where the American architect has had the most opportunities and the freest hand. Yet the small number of West Coast houses which have been included is rather misleading, for here, as we all know, California has led in both quantity and average quality.

One category which was excluded with regret was that of recent military installations. It proved to be impossible to collect sufficient material on these to make a fair selection. The omission will certainly be rectified if this exhibition of good building is repeated.

Some of the Trustees of the Museum of Modern Art felt that the Architecture Department had served its purpose by the year 1940. The architectural schools were no longer closed shops to all but traditional styles; in fact the students had practically abandoned these, even if the teaching here and there still clung to some remnants of the old methods. Why continue a crusade after it has been won? But with the trend away from the old styles has come a new type of streamlined "modernistic" that needs to be combated as vigorously as ever. The fight must go on against superficiality or sensationalism by the encouragement of sound, sincere building, as well as for wider acceptance of and interest in town and city planning.

As Alfred Barr has said, "The *battle* of modern architecture in this country is won but there are other problems with which the Department has concerned itself. Housing is one of them: another is the revaluation of the American past; and still another the development of a modern American architecture from the mingling of traditional American techniques and materials with the forms of Wright and the Europeans.

"But above these particular issues and problems is the one unending campaign which involves not merely the Department of Architecture but the Museum as a whole. This is simply the continuous, conscientious, resolute distinction of quality from mediocrity—the discovery and proclamation of excellence."

PHILIP L. GOODWIN

Architecture is more than a matter of efficient and beautiful buildings. The architect must deal with mechanical equipment, with furniture, textiles and utensils, with the space around buildings and with the relationship of one building to another. The architectural process of *rational* analysis and *creative* synthesis carries over without break into design for the crafts and for industry, and into landscaping and city planning, involving complex problems of technics and intricate social, economic and political relationships.

The modern architect sees clearly the exacting role which he must play if we are to have a more satisfactory environment, but he faces a public which is reluctant to forget the many decades in which architecture and decoration were too nearly synonymous.

Many people still prefer to entrust serious building problems to engineers, and the architect is still regarded as the man who supplies the trimmings. The attitude is no longer justified, but it persists. Any architect who applied for work in connection with the gigantic military construction program at the start of the war was apt to be told, "Oh, no, nothing for architects. We're just building here, you know. Nothing fancy." The fallacy of that argument is proved by the success of the few jobs which were given to competent architects—the Maritime Training School in San Mateo, for example (page 78).

Now, faced with the probability of large-scale construction after the war, the architect is increasingly concerned with his responsibilities. The new projects must be based on scientific analysis of present conditions and future needs. They must be sensibly planned and soundly built. They will be realized only through purposeful politics. All this depends upon the collaboration of the architect with allied technicians, and their willingness, individually and collectively, to fight for sane and decent solutions. But there is one final and unique requirement: that these projects be organized in humanly satisfactory *form*. Problems of design seem more serious than ever, even in a world at war.

International Exhibition of Modern Architecture, 1932

The point of departure chosen for this book is not so arbitrary as it sounds, for 1932 was the year of the Museum's International Exhibition of Modern Architecture. The exhibition was directed by Philip Johnson, and the accompanying catalog, now out of print, contained essays on the leading European and American architects by Henry-Russell Hitchcock, Jr., and Mr. Johnson, a separate article on housing by Lewis Mumford and a critical foreword by Alfred H. Barr, Jr., Director of the Museum. A dozen museums throughout the country each subscribed a thousand dollars toward the expenses of the exhibition.

There had been isolated articles and pictures in American magazines and the English translation (1928) of Le Corbusier's *Vers une Architecture* had aroused considerable interest, as had Mr. Hitchcock's scholarly book on *Modern Architecture* (1929), but now, for the first time in this country, popular attention was to be directed toward the exciting developments which had taken place in Europe since 1922. The Museum was not the first to point out Wright as the great architect of our time, nor to show his influence abroad, but it was the first to bring together in readily accessible form the theories and achievements of the outstanding Europeans—Le Corbusier, Mies van der Rohe, Walter Gropius and J. J. P. Oud.

Rereading the catalog after twelve years is a nostalgic experience, as it brings back the European scene of the late 'twenties and earliest 'thirties, with its magnificent work in progress and its tragically unrealized promise of new and better possibilities in art and society. Gropius is now at Harvard, Mies at the Illinois Institute of Technology. Some of their recent work is shown later in this book. Le Corbusier is still in France, probably inactive, and Oud has built nothing for years.

The choice and analysis of the principal European figures still seems remarkably valid. In their work, various as it was, and in the small number of executed buildings by their American followers, the authors found a commonly accepted discipline and vocabulary. The esthetic principles which they discerned, all "based primarily on the nature of modern materials and structure and upon modern requirements in planning," were briefly these: first, conception of a building "in terms of *volume*—of space enclosed by planes or surfaces—as opposed to mass and solidity;" second, *regularity*, or vertical and horizontal repetition as the basis of composition (rather than artificial emphasis on a central axis or on base and cornice); third, *flexibility*, particularly as expressed in the building plan; and finally, technical perfection and fineness of proportion, factors which, it was hoped, would give the values hitherto provided by applied ornament.

Le Corbusier and Pierre Jeanneret: Savoye House, Poissy-sur-Seine, France. 1929–30

Mies van der Rohe: German Pavilion at the International Exposition, Barcelona. 1929

Frank Lloyd Wright: Frederick C. Robie House, 5757 Woodlawn Ave., Chicago, Ill. 1910

Walter Gropius: Bauhaus School, Dessau, Germany. 1925–26   J. J. P. Oud: Workers' Houses, Hook of Holland. 1926–27

11

The insistence upon esthetics was particularly healthy at that time, as it deliberately opposed the highly materialistic theory of "functionalism," a credo so unrealistic that it was never actually practiced even by those who were most articulate in its support. In a period of depression the popular slogan of "functionalism" was valuable promotion for modern architecture, but it was too often used as a specious excuse for bad design.

WRIGHT'S SEPARATE POSITION

The positive influence of Frank Lloyd Wright upon the development of the new theories was carefully traced in the 1932 catalog, and his separate and unique position was sympathetically defined. His out-reaching houses, with their warm materials and their affinity with the earth, had little to do with the weightless, closed forms and cool austerities of the Europeans. The Museum's recognition of Wright's breadth and continued vitality came at a time when most of the advanced Europeans considered him the exhausted founder of a mighty tradition, a romantic pioneer without place in the carefully calculated new architecture, and few Americans accorded him even the honor due a *past* master.

PROPHECIES

Much of the Museum's criticism was prophetic. Who else at that date noticed a tendency toward the confluence of the seemingly irreconcilable architectural idioms of Wright and Le Corbusier? Other discerning observations, not generally current then: that man has a legitimate desire for monumentality, and that monumentality need not be synonymous with massive symmetry; that the trend away from the abstraction of smooth white stucco walls and toward more positive materials was a significant step towards needed enrichment; that housing and city planning were "the most essential field of modern architecture."

"VOLUME" AND "PLANE"

But the book had its weakness. Although modern materials and construction and modern living preferences were recognized as the basis of the new esthetics, there is little hint of their endless possibilities for development, nor of the effect such development would inevitably have upon design. The Museum placed great importance on "volume," achieved through non-committal, dematerialized wall planes, absence of projecting cornice, flush doors and flush ribbon windows, whereas modern architecture has always had, at least potentially, a freedom and flexibility far beyond these limits. Such devices were thoroughly characteristic only of the puristic phase of the new architecture (around 1927, the year of the Werkbund Housing Exposition in Stuttgart), and were perhaps more valid as formal symbols of Europe's idealization of the machine and the architects' interest in abstract painting than as affirmation of actual materials and construction. The over-emphasis on "volume" was confusing, as it did not seem consistent with the authors' very evident admiration for the open planning of Wright and Mies van der Rohe.

AMERICAN EXAMPLES

Turning the pages of the catalog, one is amazed by the curious assortment of American work which was included. It can now be disclosed that the Museum's trustees gave their support to the enterprise only on condition that an exact balance be preserved between the number of American and foreign architects featured in the exhibition. Therefore, in addition to Wright, the organizers of the exhibition chose the following as the best available American representatives:

Howe and Lescaze (their PSFS skyscraper, shown on page 100, is still outstanding in its field), Richard Neutra, Raymond Hood and the Bowman brothers of Chicago. Also included were buildings by Clauss & Daub, R. G. and W. M. Cory, Frederic Kiesler, Kocher & Frey, Thompson & Churchill and Oscar Stonorov.

POPULAR REACTION   The American public, amateur and professional, was strongly, if not cordially, interested in the Museum's presentation of the new architecture and in the few examples which had been built in this country. The immediate and extremely important influence was on students, to whom the new way of building came as revelation of a challenging new world. Only the most open-minded of the older architects were at all convinced. The others, already embittered by economic depression, were skeptical, or flatly hostile.

The strongest opposition came not from the traditionalists but from those powerful and successful architects who had built our "modernistic" skyscrapers with fond memories of the Paris Exposition of Decorative Arts in 1925 and the agreeable, but by then retarded, schools of Vienna, Stockholm and Amsterdam. It was they who had excluded the truly modern work from the New York Architectural League show in 1931. The answer of the progressives, among whom were members of the Museum's staff, was to picket the League with announcements of their own "Salon of Rejected Architects."

People had long found it convenient to disregard Frank Lloyd Wright, but the newest way of building they found positively offensive. Here were none of the safe, familiar things. How could one ever form a sentimental attachment for these "overgrown garages," these "cardboard boxes on stilts," these "cold white factories"? How indeed? This was the honest reaction of people who had never learned to look *directly* at a building, or a painting for that matter, without the intervention of a story. They wanted historical verisimilitude first of all, expressed as quaintness or grandiloquence. In this the American was no different from the Frenchman or the German. Ironically, here was a style which, more consciously than any other in history, was directed towards the improvement of the comfort and convenience, health and happiness of society as a whole, yet there has probably never been an architectural movement more deeply distrusted by the public.

NEED FOR HUMANIZATION   Some process of humanization was necessary before the new architecture could be whole-heartedly accepted by the average man, European or American, for even beyond his lack of understanding of architecture in general, and new forms in particular, there was genuine suspicion of the romantization of the machine which had produced these cold abstractions. Americans already suffered, if often unconsciously, from the over-mechanization of their lives, and no longer found anything romantic about it. Get up to the jangle of an alarm clock, rush through breakfast to spend an hour or two on a crowded bus or train, or driving yourself through frustrating traffic, pound a typewriter furiously all day with thirty minutes off for a counter lunch, and you're in no mood to come home to even the most beautiful *machine à habiter*. Call it escapism if you will.

New Influences

But the machine was to be a tool rather than an ideal, the means of architecture rather than its end. Outside forces encouraged a development which really unfolded from the essential strength of the movement and its inherent capacity for growth. The new European architecture opened our eyes, stimulated our minds and finally *did* materialize as an important influence on the American scene, but in conjunction with two other factors: first, a strong new interest in Frank Lloyd Wright, encouraged by his renewed creative activity in the middle and latter 'thirties; and second, a revaluation of that very dark horse—traditional vernacular building.

The young intellectuals of the 'twenties had admired the peasant geometry of Aegean and Hopi villages as well as the perfect white cylinders of grain elevators. These were forms closely related to the conscious art movements of the time. In the 'thirties there developed in the United States a new interest in more specifically native folk-architecture. Stimulated, perhaps, by Wright and by Le Corbusier's experiments with natural materials in the de Mandrot house (1930–31) and the Swiss Dormitory at the Cité Universitaire in Paris (1932–33), Americans looked again at the stone and wood barns of Pennsylvania, the white clapboard walls of New England, the low, rambling ranch houses of the West, and found them good. They were not interested in the picturesque detail of these buildings, but in their straightforward use of material and their subtle adaptation to climate and topography. Here was local encouragement for the growing international movement towards a friendlier, more differentiated contemporary architecture.

It was suddenly discovered that California had been enjoying a continuous but curiously unpublicized tradition of building in this new sense. Berkeley, for example, is full of weathered redwood houses, some built fifty years or so ago, which in spite of their eclectic detail look amazingly fresh to a modern eye. Some were from the offices of such architects as Maybeck; others were the product of anonymous carpenters and builders. Shamefully little research has been done on these important regional developments. The origins were certainly mixed, but the result was a flexible native style which could go over into modern architecture without any serious break. Wurster, for example, was producing straightforward, essentially modern houses well before 1932, based on good sense and the California wood tradition rather than on specific theories of design.

Material and Structure

In every country architects of the most varied theoretical positions have left the aggressively impersonal wall planes of the 1927 "hollow box" formula for a strong emphasis on the nature of materials in construction, and the articulation of form on a basis of widely varied types of construction. The constant example of Wright's expressive structure, even more pronounced in his work of the 'thirties—the Johnson Wax building, for example—than before, made this step particularly easy for Americans.

Many people who are responsive to architecture prefer to see a massive

Bucks County Barn (photo
Charles Sheeler, 1915)

bearing material frankly treated as such, whether it be stone, brick, adobe or concrete block. While it is technically possible, with the assistance of steel or concrete lintels, to carry these materials over wide spans, it seems more consistent either to extend the openings up to the roof or to top them with some obviously non-bearing material such as wood or light sheets of metal. A traditional example of this differentiated use of material is the Pennsylvania barn. Modern examples are the FSA housing at Chandler (page 62) and, much more dramatically, Wright's Bear Run house (page 26), with its weight-bearing core of rugged stone and its airy cantilevers of reinforced concrete.

WOOD

In their first rebound towards natural materials, architects tended to accept wood in its traditional American form—the light frame surfaced with clapboards or flush siding. One minor ground for the success of the great number of pleasant

Frank Lloyd Wright: Administration Building for S. C. Johnson & Son, Inc., 1525 Howe St., Racine, Wis. 1936–39. The hollow reinforced concrete columns taper out to become the roof itself. Glass tubes fill the intervals between the disks (photo Roy E. Petersen)

wooden houses which have been built here in the last few years is that these customary types of construction have an almost negative structural character: the supporting studs are too close together to count as a skeleton in the usual sense. As a result, the architect can work very freely, unhampered by the difficult esthetic problems which attend structural systems of more positive character.

Neutra was at first rather alone in his experiments with new types of wood construction, but before long many architects were exploring the endless possibilities of the material and creating new and appropriate forms. A major contributing factor was the development of new bonding methods whereby plywood became a serious structural rival to traditional forms of wood. Lamination at a larger scale made possible wooden trusses of amazing span (page 80). At the beginning of the war, the shortage of steel encouraged the development of new kinds of wood construction; but wood soon joined the list of critical materials.

As architects worked again with wood they began to lose that insistence on machine-like precision of finish which had been so integral a part of the original European doctrine. They delighted in the natural texture of the material and often worked from choice with rough-sawn lumber. Sometimes the effect was deliberately rustic. The reaction was inevitable, and healthy where it did not lead to inferior materials and shoddy workmanship.

The expressive treatment of materials was a new emphasis, but interest in their economical and direct use was basic in the theory of modern architecture. In the 'twenties the Germans, under the leadership of Gropius and the Bauhaus, were particularly active in the rationalization of construction as well as of plan, and early to realize the importance of standardized and interchangeable elements. Europeans have long been interested in the American development of light steel and wood construction, and welcomed such reports as Neutra's *Wie Baut Amerika?*

REASONABLE
CONSTRUCTION

(1927). With our Yankee interest in efficiency and flair for invention, and our highly industrialized society, it is remarkable that our accomplishment has not been even greater.

PREFABRICATION

It was shortly after 1932 that Americans first became romantic about prefabrication, miraculous novelty which was expected to set a depressed economy on its feet and provide satisfactory shelter even for that ill-housed "third of a nation." Actually, prefabrication had been practiced in various forms for a century, and it was not until the war brought a need for quickly erected, demountable housing that it was attempted on a basis which approached mass-production. Our experience with war housing has not proved that factory prefabrication as such has any economic advantages for general use, but it has proved that construction can be rationalized in many ways for many purposes, and that prefabrication is one of those possibilities. Inevitably, it is the *modern* architects who have led in developing more efficient methods of site use and construction.

New Structure Brings New Forms

Looking now at building methods developed in the war emergency, trends of industrial design and recent projects of the younger architects, it is evident that the skeleton no longer has its overwhelming importance of a few years back. Then, in the shift from masonry to steel or concrete frame, one thought to see a certain biological evolution from crustacean to vertebrate. Suddenly the vertebrate seems no more advanced than the new types of crustacean.

"STRESSED SKIN"

It was reinforced concrete which really started this development, but it was the use of plywood as a "stressed skin" which encouraged it. If thin sheets of plywood are properly glued or otherwise bonded, rather than nailed, to either side of a light wood frame, this full structural exploitation of the plywood "skin" gives the panel amazing strength. We are only beginning to explore the possibilities of

MOLDED FORMS

this type of construction (page 46). Plywood, plastics and metal can be molded into almost any shape, but achieve maximum rigidity in curved forms. Airplane production has been particularly responsible for experimental research in this field. If architecture is to take advantage of the possibilities of these new materials, their influence on its formal vocabulary will be startling. Perhaps the utility core of houses will be composed of such standardized elements as Buckminster Fuller's molded bathroom unit, and living space arranged with freedom (see Industrial Design section of the Museum's *Art in Progress* catalog).

THE SKELETON AND THE RIGHT ANGLE

In the 'twenties the international ideal of modern architecture was the mechanical perfection of the right angle and the parallel line. Buildings were composed throughout of clean-cut rectangles, sometimes embellished with geometrical curves. The same relentless geometry was dramatized in the site layout of the most advanced German housing projects. This rigidity no longer seems so inevitable as it did even six years ago. Counteracting influences have come from all sides.

The insistence on the rectangle in the 'twenties was symbolic of the search for social order, but it was directly occasioned by its association with what was considered the most advanced structural system, the steel or reinforced concrete skeleton. It is wholly logical that the regular network of a supporting frame be expressed in parallel walls, flat roof and rectangular openings.

And yet it was in relation to skeleton construction that the idea of the free plan was first developed. As Le Corbusier discovered in the mid-twenties, if the entire load is carried by columns, partitions can be designed with complete freedom. He proceeded to take advantage of this possibility, often finding diagonals and non-geometric curves appropriate to control the flow of human activity within the pure prisms of his buildings. Then he attacked the exterior with increasing boldness, using a curving rubble wall and a diagonal stair-tower in the Swiss Dormitory. Meanwhile, the geometry of his earlier city plans dissolved into the sinuous, contour-hugging lines of his 1930 plan for the reconstruction of Algiers. New structural systems bring new forms, to be sure, but the characteristic feeling of a time is sometimes apprehended by the artist long before the structural means are available for its realization in building. It is not coincidental that Le Corbusier is a painter as well as an architect, for the trend to organic forms affected abstract art and even Cubism well before it appeared in modern architecture.

LE CORBUSIER TAKES THE INITIATIVE—THE FREE CURVE AND THE DIAGONAL

The English followed Le Corbusier's work with interest, and the London firm of Tecton and Lubetkin was soon planning large and elegant structures in diagonals of unprecedented daring. The Aaltos of Finland, on the other hand, developed the free curve in forms appropriate to their favorite material, wood. (See list of exhibitions on page 124.)

The liberating influence of the new ideas upon this country was certainly beneficial, but the "free form" itself, a fragile phenomenon when divorced from structural and functional motivation, has been given the death kiss by over-enthusiastic designers of window displays and advertising matter.

Meanwhile Frank Lloyd Wright was also attacking the rectangle, though in very different fashion, in his 1937 "honeycomb" house in Palo Alto. The hexagon is a strict module, but the oblique planes which define the living space of this house seem remarkably unforced. At least one younger architect, influenced by this house, developed the apparent freedom of Wright's diagonals in an unexecuted series of completely non-geometric schemes.

Certainly no general dissolution of the right angle has taken place, but the architect has a new freedom of action. If the conditions of a problem invite a non-rectangular solution, he will follow it through without fear of unconventional results. The new freedom has affected both plan and elevation. It is as evident in roof-lines (page 40) as in wall-arrangement (page 32). In the 'twenties the roof was merely one of the surfaces of an enclosed volume; now it again becomes an expression of shelter. If a flat roof is used, it tends to be defined as an independent slab and projected frankly beyond the walls, casting a decisive shadow. A recessed upper floor with a cantilevered roof produces a similar effect in some multi-story buildings (pages 88 and 104). An influential prototype is Mies' Barcelona Pavilion, illustrated on page 10. But roofs are often pitched, arched, or even irregular, forms determined, or at least justified by structural logic and

A NEW FREEDOM

Lucio Costa and Oscar Niemeyer Soares, architects, with Paul Lester Wiener: Brazilian Pavilion, N. Y. World's Fair 1939 (photo F. S. Lincoln)

Sven Markelius, architect; Pomerance & Breines, associate architects: Sweden House, N. Y. World's Fair 1939 (photo Sigurd Fischer)

varying plan requirements. Here it is profitless to attempt to distinguish the example of Wright, who never completely abandoned the pitched roof, from that of the traditional vernacular; even Japanese architecture has entered as occasional inspiration. Le Corbusier's 1935 week-end house, roofed with three arched concrete vaults, side by side, must not be forgotten, nor his 1930 project for a tile-roofed house in Chile. The flat roof freed the ground plan, it is true, but it is the multi-plane roof which frees interior space.

A Human Basis for Design

Developing Sullivan's axiom—"form follows function"—the modern architect seeks in each new problem the conditions which will suggest its humanly satisfactory solution. No two problems are identical: human requirements are as various as the demands of site and climate and the potentialities of materials.

When Alvar and Aino Aalto first visited this country in 1938, heralded by the Museum's exhibition and book, they could scarcely have found a more receptive public. Our own reaction against the impersonality of the advanced European architecture of the 'twenties was paralleled by developments in other parts of the world, but particularly in Scandinavia. Aalto had been notably successful in creating fresh and sympathetic forms, based as much on intuitive understanding of the way free people might like to live as on a lively sense of the potentialities of materials and the demands of industrial production. His laminated wood furniture, now so widely distributed in the United States, is a case in point. Even more important than his encouragement of our interest in wood was his humanizing influence on more general questions of architecture and planning.

Another Scandinavian visitor who left a decisive impression on American architecture was Sven Markelius, whose Swedish Pavilion at the New York 1939 World's Fair was surely one of the beautiful buildings of our times. Everyone who saw it must remember the easy flow of space between the courtyard and the sheltered terraces, the pleasant scale, the fine and coherent way in which the wood was handled. Here again was something which Americans were quite ready to see and understand. The Brazilian Pavilion at the same Fair showed the direct influence of Le Corbusier's most recent ideas. Designed by Lucio Costa and Oscar Niemeyer Soares, it was remarkable for its open, freely curving plan, its sunbreak and its convincing Latin elegance.

The old convention of the symmetrical, rectangular plan, divided into immutable compartments, has finally been broken down, and the newer convention of the "open plan," sometimes accomplished only at considerable sacrifice of quiet and privacy, is being more thoughtfully approached. It was Aalto who made many of us more conscious of the strongly differentiated character of the modern family. His charming sketches suggested recognition of the private lives of the individuals as well as their membership in the group. Modern houses are now more apt to be articulated on the basis of group function—living, sleeping, cooking—rather than on the basis of the real unit—the person. On the other hand, the constantly changing needs of family life must literally be met with flexibility, and a one-story house with an independently supported roof and readily adjustable full-length partitions would have many advantages. Such construction has been successful in many public buildings (pages 76, 88 and 90), but its domestic use has rarely gone beyond the project stage. Flexibility and privacy must somehow be reconciled.

Aside from the varying requirements of individual families, there are many constantly recurring, standardized elements which need restudy and restatement.

LATTER-DAY INFLUENCE
FROM ABROAD

PRIVACY AND
FLEXIBILITY

EQUIPMENT

One reason for the limited success of prefabrication is that too little attention has generally been paid to the rational design of mechanical equipment, an item which represents almost a quarter of the cost of the average small house. Equipment has been *technologically* more highly developed than any other aspect of construction, but the various pieces are unintegrated, and unequal to the high functional and esthetic standards set by modern architecture. Any accomplishment in this field must be preceded by review of standards in relation to actual use. The Pierce Foundation already has such a study under way, and a number of architects are now working on designs for post-war manufacture of more efficient and better integrated bathroom and kitchen equipment.

CLIMATE

The plan of a modern building is also to a great extent conditioned by climate. Life in Puerto Rico is tolerable only if a building faces into the wind for its entire length and is blessed with complete through-ventilation. The sun is unimportant. In San Francisco, however, the strong north and northwest winds must be avoided (page 58), through-ventilation is undesirable, and the sun is welcome at every season of the year (page 32). These conditions are difficult, but have the advantage of their constancy. In the middlewest and the northeast the problem is rather more complex, as extremes of temperature make sunlight as desirable in winter as it is undesirable in summer.

The modern architect enjoys the challenge of these climatic difficulties, and welcomes them as a basis of design: the only practical alternative, after all, is complete air-conditioning. One important device, developed since 1932, is the external sunblind, so carefully calculated that it will exclude only the high, hot sun of summer. Examples will be found on pages 38, 64 and 104. In many other cases the roof itself projects as a sunblind. If we follow the brilliant example of Brazil, we will certainly make more extensive and imaginative use of such sunbreaks.

BROAD OPENINGS
TO THE SOUTH

With his passion for fresh air and sunlight, it is curious that the average American should still be somewhat reluctant to accept the broad openings to the outside which are generally characteristic of modern architecture. His most frequent objections are "too much light—the glare would hurt my eyes" and "too expensive to heat," both of which seem to have been answered by experiments conducted in a number of buildings around Chicago. The scientific experiments evidently bore out one's personal experience that light becomes unpleasant only when there is excessive contrast between light and shade: small windows cut into a dark wall will make more glare than an entire wall of glass. As for the question of heat loss, broad, double-glazed openings to the south actually result in lower-than-ordinary fuel consumption, even in the icy Chicago winters. The Lake County Sanatorium (page 92) stands as proof. The development of radiant heating has helped to make one-story buildings and extensive glass practical in even the coldest climates. Few architects have contributed as much to the development and extended application of these theories as has George Fred Keck, famous for his many "Solar" houses near Chicago.

But let no one assume that a building is modern only if it has large areas of glass.

A Building and its Setting

The relationship between building and site has also become more important in modern architecture. The principle of *volume*, stressed in the Museum's 1932 exhibition, had an implication of enclosure, but more explicitly, it was a denial of earthbound *weight*. Its perfect expression was Le Corbusier's Savoye house (page 10), lifted in proud independence of its surroundings. This was in contradiction to the position of Wright, who built close to the ground and used the broad horizontals of his cantilevered roofs to accentuate the intimacy between a building and its natural setting. The two positions then seemed irreconcilable: the one was classic and intellectual—"pure création de l'esprit" in the words of Le Corbusier; the other was romantic and emotional—"organic architecture" in the words of Wright.

WRIGHT VS. LE CORBUSIER

Only Mies van der Rohe, in such a work as the Barcelona Pavilion (page 10), seemed to find the two extremes not wholly incompatible. He proceded in a brilliant and original manner of his own which, thanks in part to the importance given it by the Museum, was received with special enthusiasm in the United States. Roof and walls, freely placed in relation to the regular pattern of the supporting columns, become independent planes intersecting to define a continuous flow of space. Here was something of Wright's emphatic shelter and lively interpenetration of space, but also a lightness, an orderliness, and a differentiation between structure and wall planes which was closely related to Le Corbusier.

That the heated controversy of Wright vs. Le Corbusier no longer seems important we owe partly to Mies, partly to our own slowly developing maturity. There are very few buildings in this book which could with any certainty be directly ascribed to the influence of either man, although there is one which was definitely inspired by Mies (page 46). Nor is the schism itself any longer so absolute. Le Corbusier's experiments with natural materials and open forms have brought him, at least superficially, closer to Wright, while the magnificent house at Bear Run (page 26) brings Wright himself considerably closer to the Europeans.

Whatever the influences—and they are many—the modern American house becomes ever more intimately related to the ground and the surrounding landscape. Living space extends into the garden and walls of glass bring the view into the house. The boundary between inside and outside becomes negligible. Sometimes the garden actually penetrates to the interior, or the house may be set against a rocky hillside (page 54). Site irregularities are welcomed.

PRIVACY

Americans have long enjoyed their front porches and their unfenced lawns and many have lived without complaint in free-standing houses on lots so narrow that the side windows of one house peer directly into those of the next. After this lengthy tradition of gregarious living, not without its positive side, we begin to appreciate the virtues of occasional privacy. On urban and suburban lots, where surroundings are often best excluded, one notices a growing number of houses planned in relation to their own enclosed courtyards. One of the earliest and most inventive, designed by Harwell Hamilton Harris and Carl Anderson, was completed in 1934. More recent examples will be found on pages 30, 46 and 50, and in the large private housing development on page 56. Sometimes the house opens almost

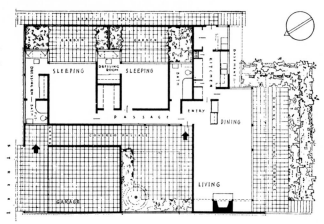

Harwell Hamilton Harris and Carl Anderson: Pauline Lowe House, Altadena, Cal. 1934

exclusively to its garden court; in other cases (pages 28, 40 and 42) the courtyard is a subtle complement to a sweeping view.

Architecture Is More Than Buildings

HOUSING
PATTERNS
RETHOUGHT

Low-cost public housing has made the architect acutely aware of the psychological and esthetic problems inherent in large-scale building. When housing was on trial in this country we tended to accept the bad along with the good in an excess of moral fervor. But now that housing is a fact, and our major source of experience for the feats of city planning which lie ahead, the more thoughtful architects and critics are questioning existing housing patterns, public as well as private, and searching for more organic solutions. If our post-war construction is not to be obsolete from the start, it must be "humanly satisfactory" in the broadest sense.

To what degree should new housing be integrated with the existing community? Is the proudly isolated development really the best answer? And isn't it socially *and* architecturally preferable to plan each neighborhood for the varied needs of many kinds of individuals and families, rather than for any one special income group and family type? The unexecuted "mixed rental neighborhood" in Washington, D. C., designed for the *Architectural Forum* by DeMars, Koch, Goldwater, Johansen and Stone, is a deliberate attack on this problem.

SITE USE

If a new community *must* be located on flat, unwooded ground, how can the result be anything but dreary? All we seem to know now is that parallel, open-ended rows of houses are *not* the answer, that every natural feature of the site must be exploited, and that any already existing buildings of interest should be retained. One interesting solution is the FSA community at Woodville (page 60). It is worth remarking here, however, that modern planning and site engineering make it feasible to build on rugged land (pages 54 and 68) rather than on the hopelessly flat ground favored by conventional builders.

UNITY AND VARIETY

If a number of private houses are to be planned as a related group, how can unity be achieved without monotony? Two answers of merit are the group at Snake Hill (page 54) and the pleasantly unpretentious houses at Glenview, Illinois, which were recently built by Schweikher, Elting and Lamb. In larger groups of lower-cost houses, public or private, the effect depends upon a precarious

23

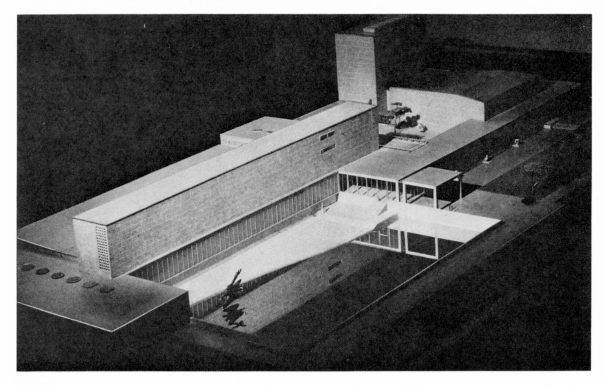

Eliel and Eero Saarinen and J. Robert F. Swanson: Model of their prize-winning design in the 1939 competition to select an architect for a proposed Smithsonian Gallery of Art, to be erected after the war on the Mall in Washington, D. C.

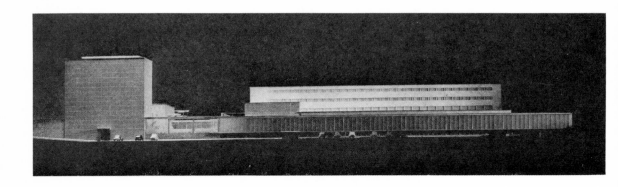

balance of repetition and variety and upon careful design and location of community buildings. Few housing projects have been as successful in this respect as those at Coatesville (page 66) and Channel Heights (pages 68 and 70).

Can decent living and working conditions be made consistent with that feeling of urbanity which many of us would hate to relinquish? Must we resign ourselves to the social vacuum of the "residential suburb," or can clean, quiet factories be included within the neighborhood area? And there is the related question as to whether an institutional effect can be avoided in large city housing schemes— a problem which is considered in Valencia Gardens (page 58).

What gives rhythm and character to a residential street? What degree of varia-

URBANITY

THE STREET

tion in form and color is desirable? Why is Fifth Avenue more exciting than Park or Madison? Why was it pleasanter to shop in the rue de Rivoli or on Bond Street than on the Champs Elysées or the Kurfürstendamm? Is a certain degree of enclosure perhaps desirable? Highways have their related problems, and it is time for us to recognize the vast dullness of the landscaping which separates and borders the beautifully sinuous road strips of our newest parkways.

These are a few of the questions which seem important today. But there is another, fervently discussed by everyone who believes in the art of architecture, and that is monumentality. Can modern architecture answer the need for buildings which will symbolize our social ideals and aspirations? Some critics believe that it not only can, but has, and point to such achievements as Le Corbusier's Swiss Dormitory and the Ministry of Education in Rio de Janeiro, and to Le Corbusier's 1927 competition project for the Palace of the League of Nations in Geneva—the project which started the controversy.

The problem became actual in 1931, in connection with Russia's international competition for a Palace of the Soviets. Before that time, the Russians had experimented with modern architecture. The awards in this competition were the first indication of their decision that only a return to the heaviest and most pompous version of neoclassicism would provide intelligible symbols of social unity.

One source of confusion seems to be the shifty word "monumentality," which cannot possibly mean the same thing in every country. A totalitarian nation demands buildings which will express the omnipotence of the State and the complete subordination of the individual. When modern architecture tries to express these things, it ceases to be modern, for modern architecture has its roots in the concept of democracy. Hitler realized this from the beginning; Mussolini tried to straddle the contradiction, with small success.

But the problem is not so quickly disposed of, as a democracy needs monuments, even though its requirements are not those of a dictatorship. There must be occasional buildings which raise the every-day casualness of living to a higher and more ceremonial plane, buildings which give dignified and coherent form to that interdependence of the individual and the social group which is of the very nature of our democracy. A building which comes close to this ideal is the project by Eliel and Eero Saarinen and J. Robert F. Swanson which received first place in the 1939 competition for a Smithsonian Gallery of Art in Washington, D. C.

The need is apparent, but the answer is still nebulous. The question of suitable scale is a delicate one, and the old arguments about ornament in modern architecture again become relevant. Can the desired effect be achieved solely through the drama of bold and imaginative structure and the richness of revealed material? More likely it will be through the complete collaboration of architect, city planner, landscape architect, painter and sculptor that the best results will be obtained. The monumental possibilities of the city square, for example, have scarcely yet been considered in modern terms. Endless discussion is possible, and healthy, but the solution will be found only in the actual trial of creation.

ELIZABETH MOCK

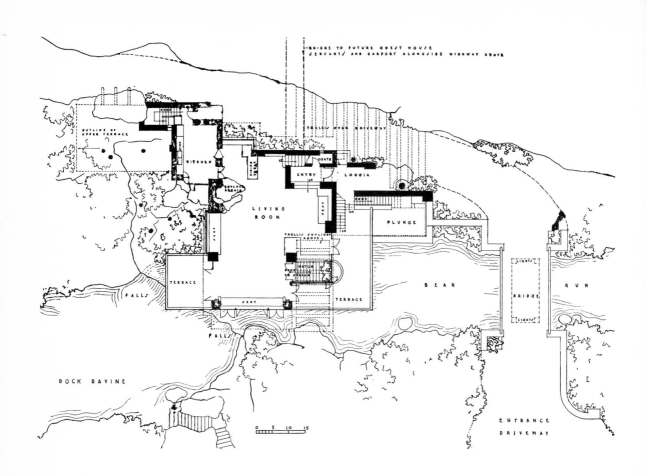

Frank Lloyd Wright: "Falling Water," house for Edgar J. Kaufmann, Bear Run, Pennsylvania. 1937-39

The lyric beauty of the house is immediate, yet some knowledge of the construction is necessary for full appreciation of the harmonious integration of material, form and setting.

The house springs out of the rocky ledges above the stream. From nearby ledges stone was quarried for the piers which rise as great uninterrupted verticals. Cantilevered from this massive core are the reinforced concrete slabs which carry the living space out over the stream.

The nature of each material becomes articulate. Stone is used only in compression, but the tensile strength of the steel rods which reinforce the concrete is exploited to the full in the airy balconies which overhang each other at various levels.

Frank Lloyd Wright: Winkler-Goetsch House, Hulett Road, Okemos, Michigan. 1939

Such easily flowing space arrangements have rarely been achieved in so compact a plan. The open sweep of the studio is emphasized by the quiet fireplace alcove and the secluded bedroom court, both shown below.

Each wall plane is distinct. There is the self-contained pattern of brick, the horizontal stripe of the redwood boards, the bands of emphatically vertical glass doors. Beneath the hovering roof slabs these planes intersect and extend to define both exterior and interior space.

The pre-assembled walls are rather like a sandwich: both sides of the plywood core are covered with building paper, faced with redwood boards, and the various layers screwed tightly together. The flat roofs, separated by a glass clearstory, are built up of crossed two-by-fours, the under sides finished with plywood. A bold cantilever shelters the carport. The house is heated by pipes coiled in loose stone beneath a concrete floor slab. All this is typical of the many small "Usonian" houses which Mr. Wright has built since 1937, but the manner in which the standard elements are handled is exceptional.

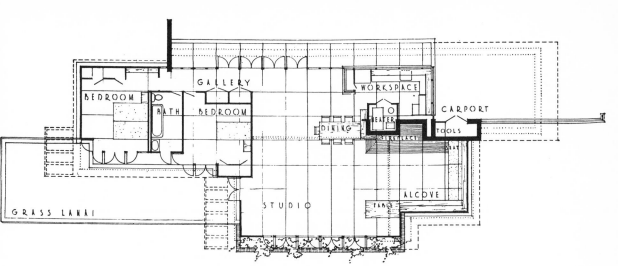

GRASS LANAI   STUDIO   BEDROOM   BATH   BEDROOM   GALLERY   DINING   HEATER   WORKSPACE   TOOLS   CARPORT   ALCOVE   TABLE

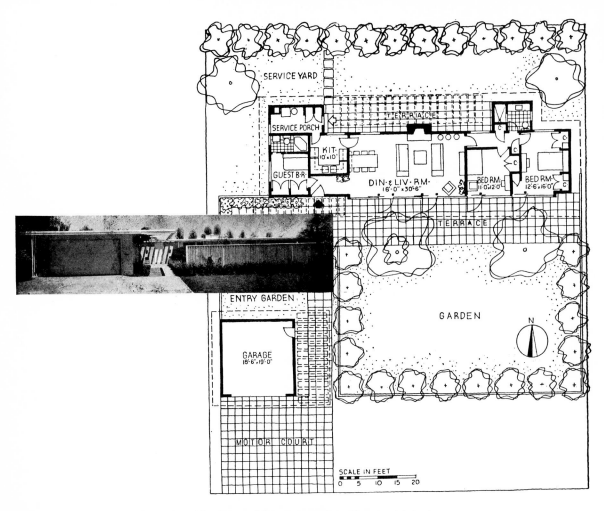

Below: Between the free-standing posts and the glass run sliding screens and a continuous curtain track.

John Funk: House for Marvin L. Heckendorf, 1815 Patricia Lane, Modesto, California. 1939

Remarkably free of personal idiosyncrasy on the part of client or architect, this inexpensive house has a classic dignity and restraint.

Two major factors influenced the design—the hot, dry climate of the San Joaquin Valley and the difficult circumstance of a lot which faced the street on the south, the most desirable exposure.

The house is set far back, shielded from the street by a sunny, fenced-in garden, and the rooms are arranged in a long, narrow block to get light and air from both sides. The entire south front opens to the garden court, yet is protected from the high summer sun by a five-foot roof overhang. The detail of this glass front is beautifully contrived.

The redwood house is painted gray, with white trim. House, garage and fence are composed in bold horizontals, extended in projecting roofs and trellises.

Above: Garden front. Most of the glass is set directly into the wooden house frame.

Entrance side, with standard metal-covered clay chimney. The rough redwood boards have weathered to a warm gray. Trim is white.

Below: View from living room to garden.

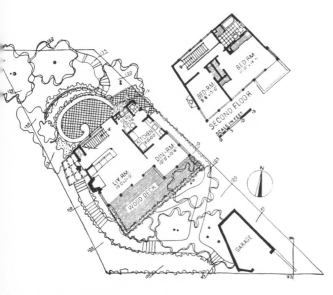

Gardner A. Dailey, architect; Marie Harbeck, landscape architect: House for L. D. Owens, 39 Atwood Avenue, Sausalito, California. 1939

Ingratiatingly modest evidence of the advantages of a flexible architecture. The architect met the problems of a wedge-shaped lot, narrow, windy and inordinately steep, with admirable directness, forsaking the characteristic horizontality of the California vernacular.

Since too much sun was impossible in that climate, the house could be designed like a wide-angle camera. Splayed side walls open up the horizontal view, and floor-to-roof glass on two sides gives full vision **down** to San Francisco Bay and **up** to the almost vertical garden which rises behind the house like a curving tapestry.

33

Harwell Hamilton Harris: House in Fellowship Park, 2311 Fellowship Parkway, Los Angeles, California. 1935

A capacious low-hipped roof shelters a tiny hillside house of extraordinary freshness and charm. The designer was also the client, and he and his wife wanted only the bare bones of domesticity—just a large space for living and sleeping, a bathroom and a kitchen. But the appearance of simplicity is deceptive, as it is the product of refinement rather than of primitivity.

The wooded hill is scarcely disturbed, for cutting and filling were avoided by the use of concrete pier foundations. The roof rests on a series of widely spaced posts, braced by ingenious flying buttresses of wood and iron. Between the posts slide doors glazed alternately with clear and frosted glass. In good weather the doors are removed on three sides and the living room becomes an open pavilion, confronting ferns and oak trees and the distant view of mountains.

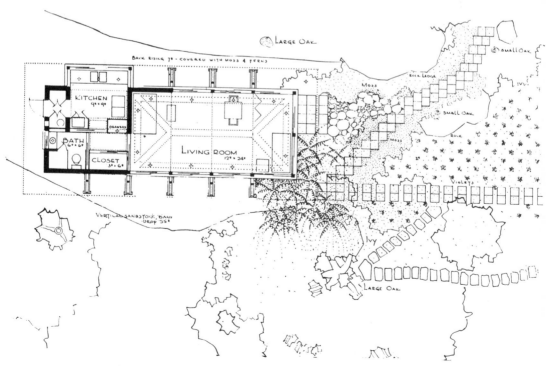

Walter Gropius and Marcel Breuer: House for Henry G. Chamberlain, Castle Hill Road, Wayland, Massachusetts. 1940

A weekend house of informal plan, ingenious construction and immaculate elevations.

The wooden superstructure is lightly poised above a rough stone basement. The stud walls themselves act as trusses: strengthened with diagonal boarding and with interior and exterior finish of tongue-and-groove fir sheathing, their rigidity is such that no heavy beams were required for the eight-foot projection of living room and kitchen, no heavy lintels for the broad window openings.

The suspended staircase is similar in principle, but composed of three layers of tongue-and-groove boarding.

A carefully calculated roof projection shelters the large south-facing window.

Exteriors are beautifully proportioned. The cut-out window openings would be meaningless in relation to the isolated supports of skeleton construction; but in this case they are a direct expression of the continuously stressed wall surfaces.

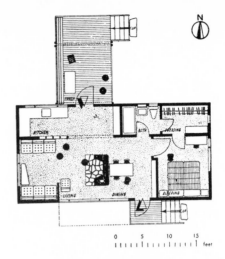

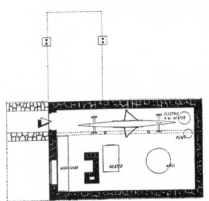

Right: View from living room through kitchen alcove to porch.

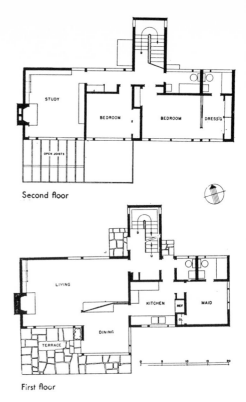

Second floor

First floor

The vertical shaft of the stair, foreign to the regular framing pattern of the two floors, is articulated as a separate wing. Notice also the economical arrangement of four bathrooms on one plumbing stack.

Walter Gropius and Marcel Breuer: House for James Ford, Wood's End Road, Lincoln, Massachusetts. 1939

The plan is superbly rational. Disposition of rooms in one narrow block, unbroken by a stair well, means that single, uninterrupted rows of joists can cover the uniform span. A second advantage is that all major rooms can face the south and overlook an adjacent forest.

The projecting blinds which shield the broad windows from the high summer sun are a lively accent to the smooth white-boarded walls.

The house is gracious in scale, and the living room has a fine and easy flow of space. Smoothly joined panels of gray-painted plywood cover ceiling and walls.

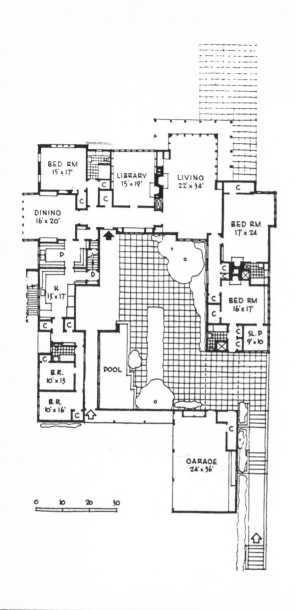

John Yeon, designer; A. E. Doyle & Associate, architects: House for A. R. Watzek, S. W. Skyline Boulevard, Portland, Oregon. 1937

A house intimately related to its magnificent natural setting. From the entrance drive the harmonious arrangement of low-pitched roofs (above) is a subtle echo of the distant view of Mount Hood.

A gate leads to the fore-court, where a loggia opens to a delightful garden. The free forms of trees and shrubs are skilfully related to the geometry of pool and flagging and the silvery gray walls of the house.

The interior has a conventional formality unrelated to the exterior. All major rooms open widely to the view at the east, where the landscaping is appropriately bold and uncomplicated.

Edward D. Stone: House for A. Conger Good-year, Wheatley Hills Road, Old Westbury, Long Island, New York. 1940

Floor and roof slab are the positive elements. The supporting structure, brick or wood bearing walls and steel lally columns, seems incidental.

A famous art collection is shown to advantage, without sacrifice of domestic scale. In its glass-walled gallery (left) it becomes part of the tranquil closed garden through which one enters the house.

On the opposite side are the living and bed-rooms, open to the paved terrace, the swimming pool, and the gentle countryside beyond. Glass stretches the full width and height of each room. Floor and ceiling continue out, interrupted only by the narrow steel frame of the glass, and there seems to be no exact boundary between interior and exterior.

Above and below: living room.

1. Servant's Room   2. Kitchen   3. Pantry   4. Dining Room   5. Study
6. Living Room 7. Guest Room 8. Bedroom 9. Dressing Room 10. Gallery

George Howe: House for Clara Fargo Thomas, Mount Desert Island, Maine. 1939

Limited in this isolated spot to native craftsmanship and traditional materials, the architect worked through these potential obstacles to a thoroughly modern solution which yet seems easy and inevitable on the rugged Maine coast.

The living room, lifted by a local bridge-builder's double concrete cantilever, stretches out over Somes Sound and opens on three sides to a view of sea and sky and wooded islands. Other rooms are arranged in long wings on the hill above, parallel with the rocky shore.

Square wooden posts, spaced ten feet apart, support emphatic double-pitched roofs. Roof and ceiling form a clean triangle, as the lintels are placed above the flush ceiling, and deep eaves give an assurance of shelter. Roof slopes are covered with silvery shingles, while ceilings and under-eaves are painted an atmospheric gray-blue.

The intervals between posts are filled with floor-to-ceiling panels of glass. Some are fixed in place; others slide back to leave only a narrow railing between interior and exterior. The windowless walls are covered with oiled cedar clapboards.

View from the bedroom wing.

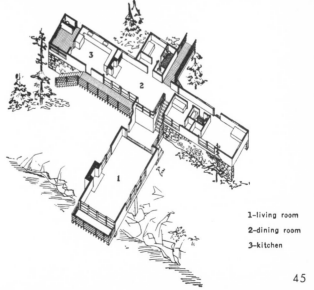

1–living room
2–dining room
3–kitchen

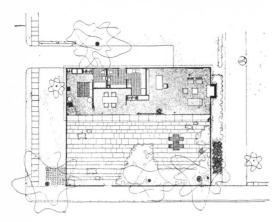

Philip Johnson, architect; S. Clements Horsley, associate: House for Philip Johnson, 9 Ash Street, Cambridge, Massachusetts. 1942

A house of classic serenity and ascetic luxury, designed to meet the special tastes of its bachelor owner. House and garden are one space, defined and protected by an enclosing square of wall and separated from each other only by clear glass. Openness and privacy are reconciled by curtains. The rhythmic flow of space from one part of the house to another and out to the garden court is vivid counterpoint to the closed form of the exterior—startling and ungregarious on its conventional open-lawned New England street.

Walls of house and garden are prefabricated four by nine foot plywood panels and the panel ceiling is partially supported by laminated wood columns and beams.

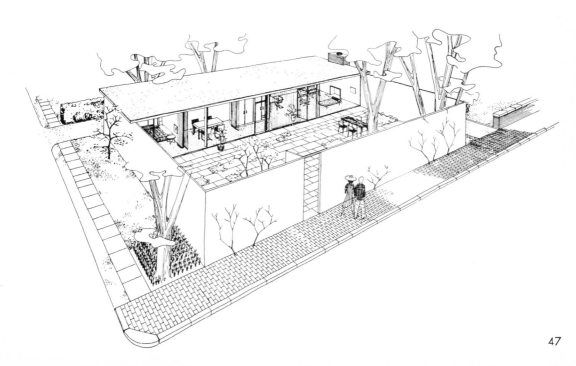

47

Vincent G. Kling: House for A. J. Peaslee, Mantoloking, New Jersey. 1941

The living room was elevated for a better view over the ocean to the southeast and Barnegat Bay to the northwest. Between this main block and the pair of bathhouses a row of bedrooms, surrounded by balconies, bridges over an outdoor dining terrace. The house is of wood, with plywood sheathing, but the broader spans and bolder cantilevers are strengthened with steel.

Bright sunlight reveals the usual seasidehouse as a bland, undifferentiated mass, its detail too small to count in terms of light and shade. The vigorous, plastic exteriors of this house owe much of their character to the play of the high-lighted horizontals of roof and balcony against their own deep shadows.

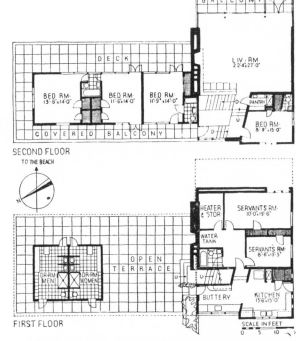

48

SERVICE
KITCHEN · PANTRY · PASSAGE
PATIO
LAV.
ENTRANCE · HALL · DUMB. WTR. · UP · DN · DINING RM. · STUDY · LAV.

FIRST FLOOR PLAN

LIBRARY · LIVING RM. · TERRACE
DUMB WTR. · UP · DN

SECOND FLOOR PLAN

Street façade.   Garden façade from study roof.

William Lescaze: House for Edward A. Norman, 124 East 70th Street, New York, N. Y. 1941

A town house which makes the best of one of New York's typical and absurd twenty-foot lots.

The plan of the ground floor is pleasantly introvert. The dining room opens upon a garden court, planted with ginkgo, flowering hawthorn, dogwood and crab-apple, and skirted by the glazed passage which leads to a well secluded study.

Living rooms are on the floor above, running from one end of the house to the other with a fine, easy flow of space, every detail carefully subordinated to the rhythm of the whole. Facing the garden and the south is an entire wall of glass, shown above, slanted to trap the sun and to create an illusion of a more generous interior. The roof of the ground-floor passage and study becomes a landscaped terrace; from the living room one sees an asymmetrical arrangement of raised flower boxes silhouetted against the great blank wall of the building beyond. Above the living floor are the bedrooms.

The street façade is suitably urbane, pleasantly proportioned and well-scaled in relation to its neighbors. The relationship between clear glass and insulating glass block, always difficult, is most satisfactorily solved on the third floor. The white brick walls are relieved by the entrance recess of gray brick and the chrome yellow door.

51

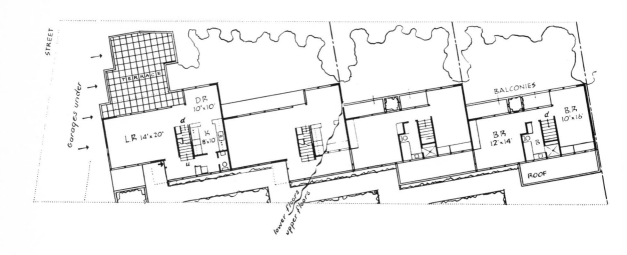

Gregory Ain: Dunsmuir Flats, 1281 South Dunsmuir Avenue, Los Angeles, California. 1939

By staggering the four row houses on his difficult 49-foot inside lot, the architect has gained extraordinary advantages. Major rooms have three exposures and each house obtains a well screened garden court, each bedroom a secluded balcony. The houses open to their gardens on the south, but windows on street and entrance sides are kept high for privacy.

The building is as consequent in structure and form as it is in plan. Instead of the usual stud frame, widely spaced 4-by-4 wood posts are the basis of an extremely regular design. Glass is set directly between the posts, forming continuous bands almost flush with the smooth walls. Emphasis is on the enclosed volume rather than on the walls which define it.

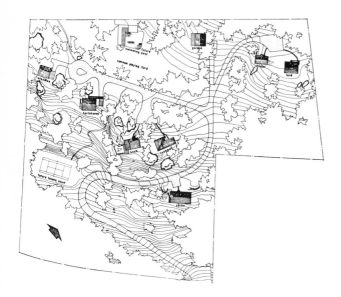

The houses are built against the steep slopes which rim the tract, leaving the relatively flat land at the center as garden and play space, used in common by all houses.

Group of eight houses on Snake Hill, Belmont, Massachusetts. Carl Koch: original development, 1940. Carl Koch, Huson Jackson and Robert Kennedy: three "Cemesto" houses, 1942

Group land purchase, reasonable site layout and imaginative architecture have brought out of a steep hillside, distrusted by conventional builders, the liveliest and most livable group of inexpensive houses in the East.

The original houses are of native stone and wood frame, covered with narrow boards of unpainted fir. Details are refreshingly simple, but durability has at times been sacrificed to economy. Most successful, and most unusual, is the Koch house (below right), which climbs down the cliff on three levels. Interiors are shown on the page opposite.

The later houses are a modern version of medieval half-timber. The exposed frame is filled in with insulated panels of asbestos cement.

Entrance of a "Cemesto" house.

Entrance of the Koch house.

Above: The workroom of the Koch house is partially walled with the exposed rock of the hillside itself.
Below: The Koch living room, with its superb view over Boston.

Baldwin Hills Village, Rodeo Road near La Brea Avenue, Los Angeles, California. Reginald D. Johnson and Wilson, Merrill & Alexander, architects; Clarence S. Stein, consulting architect. 1942. (FHA limited-dividend rental development, 627 units)

This private housing scheme is all the more remarkable when one knows the tenacity with which FHA has fought the advantages of modern architecture and modern site-planning, time and again proven by low-cost public housing. The major differences between this and the rather less costly public projects are increased spaciousness, inside and out, more extensive landscaping, individual garages and private patios (below).

The community forms one gigantic block, fringed with "garage courts" and centered with a "village green" from which finger parks and footpaths penetrate to every part of the development. The houses are attractive, though undistinguished. Their patios face the garage courts and they open widely to park strips on the opposite side. Community facilities include a club house, child care center, fenced play areas, tennis and badminton courts.

Schools are near and an adjoining shopping center is planned.

Second floor

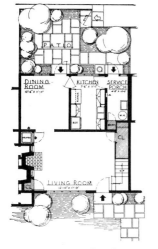

First floor

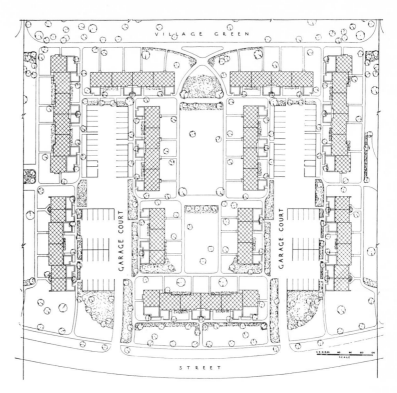

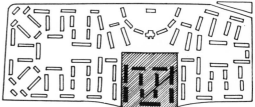

The hatched area indicates that shown at larger scale.

Valencia Garden, Valencia Street at 15th, San Francisco, California. Harry A. Thomsen, Jr., and William Wilson Wurster, architects; Thomas D. Church, landscape architect. 1943 (Started as a USHA low-rent project, 246 units).

Outstanding among urban housing schemes for its easy livability and the logic of its site plan, Valencia Gardens has little of the institutional atmosphere which haunts many of the others. The occasional starkness of the façades makes the general cheerfulness all the more remarkable.

To discourage the prevailing north and northwest winds from sweeping through the project, the apartment buildings were arranged to form three garden and two service courts. Since these courts were necessarily deep, the architects emphasized their breadth by interrupting the long side walls with balconies which serve the smallest apartments as entrance corridors and sheltered sitting space, and by using color to point up the breaks in the building line. The concrete walls are gaily painted in terra cotta, blue, sand and bright yellow. The base is dark green.

In the garden courts the illusion of width was furthered by the independent forms of the island gardens, the diagonals of the pavement, and the choice of many-forked, round-headed trees. Pavement predominates for varied use and low upkeep, but an impression of abundant greenery is given by the elevated gardens, especially when seen from normal eye-level. Raised beds are no novelty in themselves, but their use in connection with low-rent city apartments is both new and sensible. Some are covered with grass, some with prostrate juniper, and many ar e dotted with trees—Victoria box and eucalyptus. The brick retaining walls make excellent seats and discourage short-cuts through the gardens.

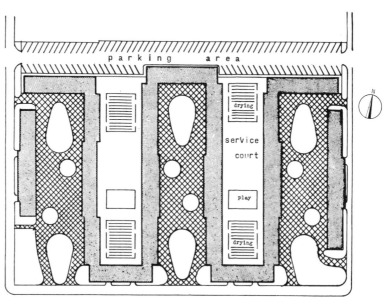

Rural community, Woodville, California. Farm Security Administration: Vernon DeMars, architect, with Butts, Eckbo, Edie, Steiner, Sweeting, Thompson, Williams and Yuasa; Nicholas Cirino, site engineer, with Beamer, Clark, Crenshaw, Davis, Donaldson, Kelly, Stark and Verag. 1941

The design of a community is seldom the work of an individual: its success as architecture depends on the skill of the collaborating designers and technicians and on the ability of the architect and engineer who coordinate the group effort.

Woodville is handicapped by a flat, bare site, but its completeness makes it one of the most interesting of the FSA communities. As in many of the others, metal shelters (background of airview) are provided for migrant agricultural workers as well as more comfortable single and row houses for resident farmers. The row houses are similar to those at Yuba City, shown on the next page.

But houses alone do not make a community. The two top pictures show the lavatory unit and the laundry and shower building, both for campers. Below are store, nursery, and interior and exterior of the clinic. The cleanly articulated wings of the large building on the opposite page house elementary and nursery schools, social center and administrative offices.

These handsome buildings are the result of careful and economical design: FSA's San Francisco office has shown that "bureaucratic architecture" can also be distinguished.

South side of Chandler housing.

Agricultural workers' community, Chandler, Arizona. Farm Security Administration: Burton D. Cairns and Vernon DeMars, architects. 1936-37 (32 units)

Where traditional materials and techniques best meet the conditions of a problem, the modern architect welcomes them gladly as the basis of his design. These houses are of adobe, or sun-baked blocks of mud and straw, for centuries the standard structural material of the hot, dry Southwest.

The south façades are a brilliant example of sensible, sensitive use of a massive building material. The thick adobe walls which separate and support the houses project to enhance the actual and apparent privacy of each dwelling. The cellular effect which results is for this reason perhaps a more direct and desirable treatment of the row-house façade than the unbroken horizontals of more conventional solutions.

Exterior walls, supporting nothing, are appropriately light and open. On either side of the sleeping floor is a double row of ventilating flaps, the lower of plywood, the upper of translucent glass-substitute. Upper story, roof and transverse walls all project on the south to shield the houses from excessive sun.

Compare these houses with the FSA housing at Yuba City, California, shown below. Program and climate are almost identical, but the use of wood rather than adobe has resulted in a very different, though no less distinguished appearance.

Below: Two views of housing at Yuba City, California.

Above: Chandler housing. South side.

Chandler housing. Above: North side. Below: Plans and section.

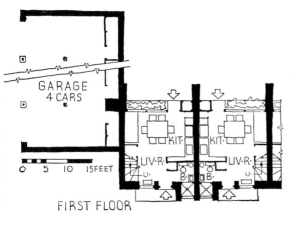

GARAGE 4 CARS

KIT· KIT·

LIV·R· LIV·R·

0 5 10 15 FEET

FIRST FLOOR

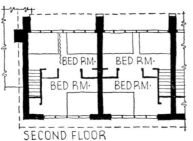

BED RM· BED RM·

BED RM· BED RM·

SECOND FLOOR

B·R· SLEEP. PORCH

KITCHEN

SECTION

Hugh Stubbins, Jr.: Housing at Windsor Locks, Connecticut. 1942 (FWA Division of Defense Housing, 85 units)

The circle is theoretically the most economical building form, as it has least peripheral wall in relation to its area. More practical than the circle and only slightly less economical is the square, which is why so many minimum houses have square plans.

It would be difficult to find a more distinguished version than the two-bedroom unit developed for Windsor Locks. Plan and sketch are shown on the opposite page. Each inch of the 26-foot square is effectively used. The zig-zag relationship of the dining corner, kitchen and utility space gives a sense of privacy and spaciousness, yet achieves a maximum of convenience. Bedrooms are tiny, but planned for efficient use. All the mechanical equipment for kitchen, heating and bathroom has been concentrated in one compact unit. Coal is used for heating, cooking and hot water.

Windows have been carefully studied. Next to the casements are fixed panes of glass, set directly into the structural members. A row of such windows, protected by an adjustable sunblind, seems to add space and scale to the small living room.

The larger houses (left, the two bottom pictures) are identical in plan but for an extra projecting bedroom. Some of the houses are joined in pairs, and all are arranged diagonally on the flat un-wooded site to allow each one a view beyond the walls of its immediate neighbors.

The same care went into construction: side walls and roof trusses were assembled separately on the ground and quickly raised into place on the concrete floor slab. The square plan meant that trusses of identical design could be used to make roof slopes in either direction.

The severity of the precise exteriors is relieved by the vertical redwood siding, the well-proportioned window openings, and the gay white-painted wooden sunblinds, but the project suffers from the drabness of its site. Landscaping on war housing projects has been drastically cut.

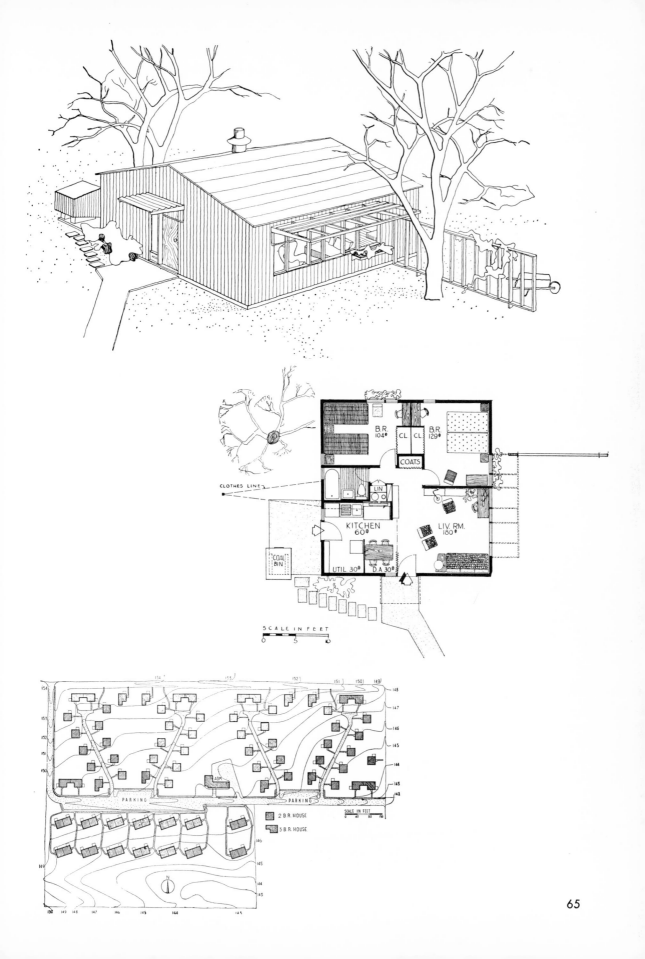

B.R.
104⁰

CL CL

B.R.
129⁰

COATS

CLOTHES LINE

LIN

KITCHEN
60⁰

LIV. RM.
180⁰

COAL
BIN

UTIL 30⁰

D.A 30⁰

SCALE IN FEET
0   5

PARKING

PARKING

ADM

SCALE IN FEET
0   40   80   120

☐ 2 B.R. HOUSE
■ 3 B.R. HOUSE

N

Howe, Stonorov & Kahn: Carver Court, Coatesville, Pennsylvania. 1944. (Permanent public war housing—FPHA)

A road leaves the Coatesville-Paoli highway to make a single elongated loop on a lightly wooded hillside. Grouped about the strip of park at its center are houses for a hundred colored war workers and their families. At the base of the loop is a brick-and-wood building (bottom, left) which combines administrative and maintenance offices with a nursery play-room (at right of picture), used also as a social center for adults.

The scale is intimate. In every part of the community one is pleasantly aware of the shape and substance of the whole.

Buildings have been skilfully arranged to preserve and enhance the natural character of the site. Of the four dwelling types, the least usual is the elevated three-bedroom unit shown below and on the opposite page. Living and sleeping rooms are raised on transverse walls of concrete block. The entrance is beneath, with heater and storage space, but the greater part of the ground area is free for use as carport and sheltered terrace.

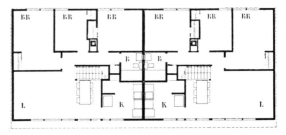

1ST

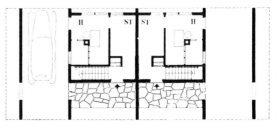

G.F.

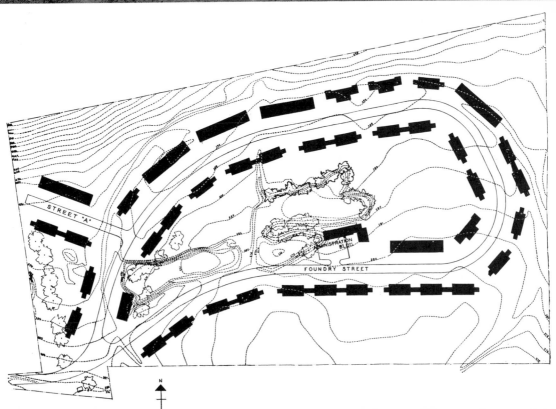

Channel Heights, San Pedro, Los Angeles, California. Richard J. Neutra, architect; Lewis Eugene Wilson, consultant, 1943. (FPHA permanent war housing, 600 units)

Close to shipyards and harbor and adjacent to a fine public park, the 160-acre site also offers splendid views over valley and ocean. But the land could not have been used without modern site engineering and machinery, as it rises some 245 feet from east to west and is cut through by ravines, bisected by a 90-foot canyon.

The steep slopes have been laid out in great blocks, unbroken by noisy, hazardous through-streets, and are planned for 3.7 families per acre, an extremely low density. Houses are laid at an angle to the dead-end streets which indent the "superblocks" and connect with the peripheral highways. A continuous park area flows through the village and foot-paths lead safely from one part to another, as highway danger is eliminated by three pedestrian underpasses.

Complete community facilities have been planned and thus far there is a community building and child-care center (opposite page and top left), a shopping center (second from top) and a garden craft center (third from top). Equipped with nursery, lath house and plant dispensary, the garden center encourages gardening as healthy recreation for children and adults and has already affected the appearance of the project.

The community is remarkably free of monotony. One reason is the superb site, but another is the variety and distinction of the houses and the skill with which they are grouped (see following pages). Most of the houses are single story and all are planned for unobstructed view. Their pre-cut, pre-fitted wooden frames are covered on the exterior with unpainted redwood and cement plaster. The gently sloping roofs, so prominent as one looks down from the higher parts of the project, are covered with a natural-colored gravel much like the surface of the winding walks.

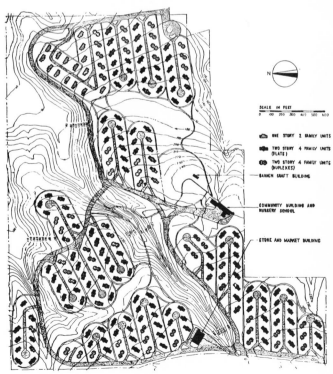

ONE STORY 2 FAMILY UNITS

TWO STORY 4 FAMILY UNITS
(FLATS)

TWO STORY 4 FAMILY UNITS
(DUPLEXES)

GARDEN CRAFT BUILDING

COMMUNITY BUILDING AND
NURSERY SCHOOL

STORE AND MARKET BUILDING

SCALE IN FEET
0 100 200 300 400 500 600

N

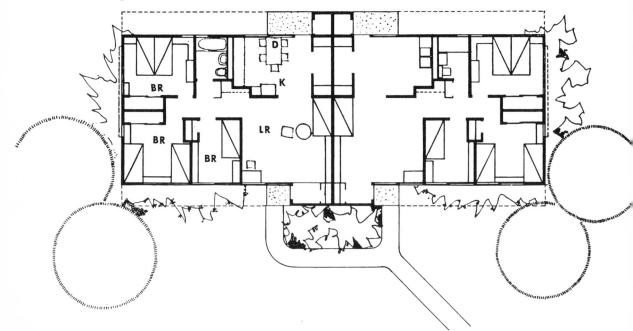

Opposite page: Plan and interior of the three-bedroom twin houses shown above. The furniture was designed by the architect.

Right: Each block is a row of four two-bedroom houses. Balconies are placed where they will get the best possible view.

Richard J. Neutra: Experimental School, Bell Avenue at Bear Avenue, Los Angeles, California. 1935

Built as an addition to an existing school, this carefully studied arrangement of classrooms and kindergarten has been recognized as a classic in its field.

Each classroom gets light and air from two sides, through high windows over the covered passage and through a great wall of glass at the west, where sliding doors open to an outdoor class area. Walls and roof project to exclude rain, over-abundant sunlight and the noise of neighboring classrooms, and external canvas sunblinds can give additional protection. The kindergarten, however, deliberately faces the south and the sun.

The light wood frame was specially designed for earthquake safety, and the deep wood-truss roof is ventilated by louvered openings in its tapered over-hangs.

The horizontality of the east side of the building, emphasized by the lightly supported canopy of the passage, contrasts with the west side, where classrooms are expressed as a repetition of wholly distinct units.

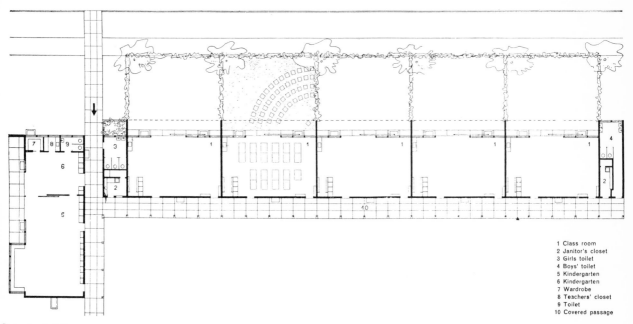

Floor plan 1:300

1 Class room
2 Janitor's closet
3 Girls toilet
4 Boys' toilet
5 Kindergarten
6 Kindergarten
7 Wardrobe
8 Teachers' closet
9 Toilet
10 Covered passage

Eliel and Eero Saarinen; Perkins, Wheeler and Will: Crow Island Elementary School, Willow Road, Winnetka, Illinois. 1940

Modern education is directly concerned with the psychological well-being of children, yet few educators realize the relevance of a sympathetic architectural environment. The Winnetka Board of Education, however, wanted a school which would actually contribute to the results of their famous educational system, not only through efficiency, but through encouragement of the child's sense of freedom and security. They realized that such a program called for modern architecture.

After studying the teaching method, the architects designed the model classroom shown opposite. The site plan shows how the building was developed from this relatively self-sufficient unit. Different age-groups are in separate wings, each with its outdoor play area. Offices and library are at the center, with playroom and auditorium. Details are heavy, but the general scale is pleasant.

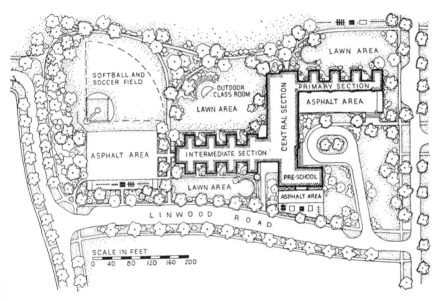

Each friendly classroom has its workshop, lavatory and garden court. Two walls are glass, two faced with natural wood. The light wooden furniture was specially designed by the architects.

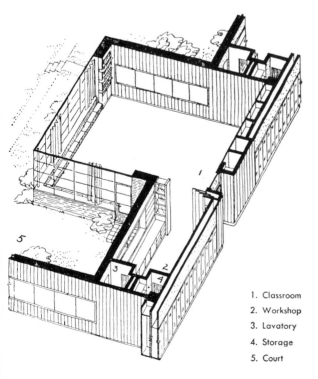

1. Classroom
2. Workshop
3. Lavatory
4. Storage
5. Court

Franklin & Kump and Associates: Acalanes Union High School, Lafayette, California. 1940-41

The complex functions of the large rural high school were carefully analyzed, and competently solved in a building as handsome as it is sensible. The dispersed plan is thoroughly practical in this climate.

Students come by bus or automobile, and the five-hundred-foot loading platform at right of the airview serves also as a sheltered passage to connect cafeteria, workshops and gymnasium, all conveniently grouped for use by adults as well as by children. There is no "entrance façade."

A cross-passage leads to the one-story, parallel rows of classrooms shown at the left of the airview. Each row is essentially a long, open loft, divided into rooms by easily adjustable plywood partitions. Three more rows have now been added on the far side of the passage.

Two-sided light makes better vision. In addition to the continuous glass on the north, there are high windows over the corridors on the south.

Lockers are in the open passage which connects the classrooms.

Below: In the foreground is the cafeteria with its terrace for outdoor lunches. Workshops are behind, and the arched concrete structure in the rear is the gymnasium. All are connected by a canopied passage. Parking space is at the right.

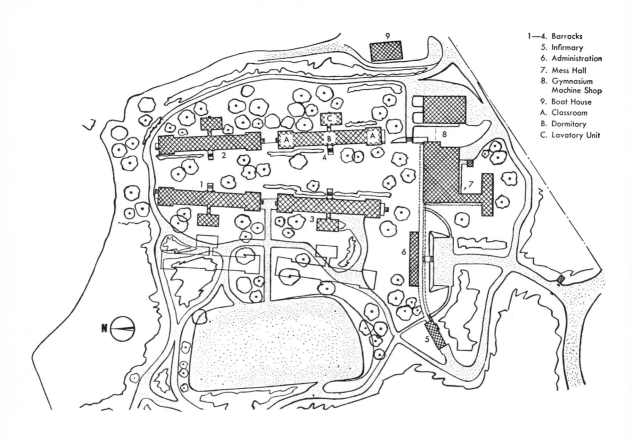

1—4. Barracks
  5. Infirmary
  6. Administration
  7. Mess Hall
  8. Gymnasium
     Machine Shop
  9. Boat House
  A. Classroom
  B. Dormitory
  C. Lavatory Unit

Below left: Differences in the level of barrack and separate lavatory unit are cared for by the glazed connecting ramp.

Below right: Barrack entrance with classroom projecting at the end. Note the stepped roofs.

Gardner A. Dailey: U. S. Merchant Marine Cadet Basic School, Coyote Point, San Mateo, California. 1942

It is unusual to find emergency military construction in which design has been adjusted to site rather than site to design. Extensive grading operations were avoided by stepping down the buildings as the land falls away to the water. This was facilitated by concrete pier foundations and by the articulation of various sections of the buildings for separate adjustment to the ground slope. Each barrack is symmetrical in plan, as it is used by two cadet groups.

The eucalyptus trees were retained for camouflage and amenity, and their tall shafts accentuated by the low-pitched roofs and the canopied walks which connect mess hall, administrative offices and infirmary. The wooden buildings, skilfully planned for easy and quick (two months) construction in the simplest of standard materials, are distinguished by their casual good looks, and the school as a whole has an unregimented orderliness which is refreshing.

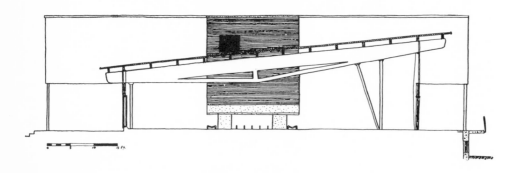

Skidmore, Owings & Merrill: Main Reception Building, Great Lakes Naval Training Station, Great Lakes, Illinois. 1942

Here service men can meet their visitors under extraordinarily pleasant circumstances. There is nothing of the sense of barren exposure which one might expect in a hall of 60 by 190 feet.

The roof construction is unusual. Trusses of unpainted laminated wood (see section) are supported at either end by light steel columns, and the long walls, carrying nothing, become protective screens of glass and vertical fir boarding. On the street side (left), the west, there is only a high strip of window; but the roof tilts up toward the east, where a floor-to-ceiling wall of glass looks out over a cantilevered concrete terrace to a ravine. An open-sided concrete and brick fireplace suggests a division between reception space and lounge.

The long horizontals of the exterior are crisply terminated by a transverse block of offices elevated at one end of the building.

Lawrence B. Anderson and Herbert L. Beckwith: Swimming pool, Massachusetts Institute of Technology, Cambridge, Massachusetts. 1940

At last the swimming pool emerges from its traditional cellar and takes its place in the sun.

The pool faces the sun-bath garden and the south with a great wall of fixed glass. Ideally, the glass would slide back in warm weather: actually, only a small door opens to the garden. Other windows are high behind the spectators' gallery. Coils for radiant heating are set in pool decks and ceiling. Present locker rooms are temporary.

Pools are lined with brownish-purple tile, and decks are gray with dull black curbs. Markers and window seat are lemon yellow tile and the acoustic plaster of walls and ceiling is a light gray. The colorful furniture behind the diagonally inset glass wall of the coaches' office is added gaiety.

The steel frame is coated with a heavy, noncommittal finish of buff brick; but the copper spandrel over the great window is suitably light and the detail throughout is crisp and fresh.

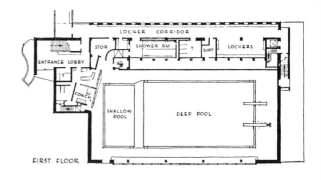

FIRST FLOOR

Frank Lloyd Wright: Taliesin West, Maricopa Mesa, Paradise Valley, near Phoenix, Arizona. 1938-

A great and poetic building designed in subtle harmony with its magnificent setting of desert and mountains, and with deep intuitive feeling for the nature of the chosen materials and for the way man might best live under the hard, bright Arizona sun.

Taliesin West is the winter home and workshop of Mr. Wright and his students, and was built almost entirely by the students themselves. Walls are concrete, but of a special kind: native boulders, red, yellow and gray, were laid in rough wooden forms and cement poured over. Above these colorful, variously tapered walls are the great redwood trusses which support canvas-covered roof flaps. Glass is unnecessary, as the canvas admits a softly diffused light.

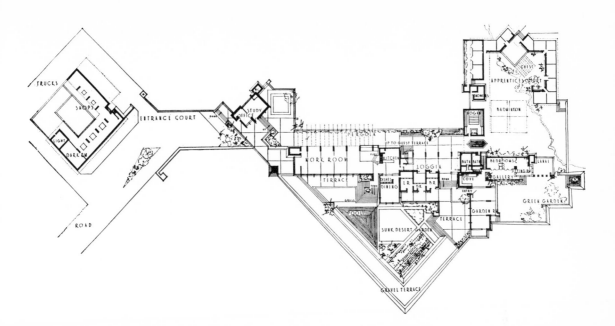

Above: View past Mr. Wright's office to the pergola and the large work room. This work room (below) serves also as a general living room.

Burnham Hoyt: Red Rocks Amphitheatre for Denver, at Morrison, Colorado. 1941

Fourteen miles west of the city, beyond the first foothills, is Denver's Park of the Red Rocks, famous for its huge, intensely red sandstone monoliths. Their forms are varied and fantastic, often lifting toward the west at a 30° angle. Between two of the largest, two and three hundred feet high respectively, lay a rough natural amphitheatre with extraordinarily good acoustics.

Transformation into a workable theatre for 9,000 people took four years. With full realization that the best architecture would be in this case the least architecture, reshaping and new construction were reduced to a minimum, and so successfully subordinated to the setting that one is scarcely aware of conscious design.

The natural shape of the ground allowed sufficient distance between the rows of benches for circulation, with radiating aisles only at the side. Storage and dressing rooms are beneath the stage and parking areas out of sight and earshot of the audience.

Philip L. Goodwin and Edward D. Stone: The Museum of Modern Art, 11 West 53rd Street, New York, N. Y. 1939

A few years ago an art museum was a repository for static collections. Almost any pompous building served. Today's problem is to provide for constantly changing exhibitions and an expanding program of public services. A building must first of all be flexible.

Here steel and concrete columns take the load, and partitions can be shifted at will on every floor. A maximum of free space was obtained by concentrating fixed elements such as stairs, elevators, air ducts and lavatories at one end.

The entrance façade (left) has little to do with floor and ceiling levels and ignores the vertical shaft of the staircase, yet has dramatic appeal of its own. The ground floor is separated from the street only by clear glass. Above are the two main gallery floors, with walls of translucent insulating glass. Then come two stories of offices and the pierced roof slab of the members' penthouse. Walls are hung with white marble and blue tile.

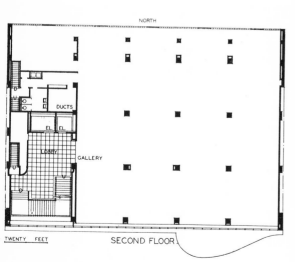

SECOND FLOOR

TWENTY FEET

Above: Members' penthouse. The flat, pierced walls of Rockefeller Center are as much a part of the room's decoration as the exotic plant forms.

Right: Basement auditorium. Undulating walls and ceiling are the result of acoustical calculations.

Left: The north wall of the second floor is glass brick, interspersed with clear glass for a view over the sculpture garden.

The rear of the building.

The main entrance.

Franklin & Kump and Associates: City Hall, Fresno Street, Fresno, California. 1941

Looking back to the dubious position of modern architecture in this country in 1932, it seems incredible that it took only nine years to penetrate to that stronghold of American conservatism, the city hall. The citizens of Fresno were at first somewhat dismayed by their novel acquisition, but have learned to appreciate its efficiency, its lack of nonsense, the beauty of its simple materials and the dramatic importance of its fine entrance hall.

Ramps replace stairs in this unusual building. Their sweeping diagonals enliven the two-story entrance hall which bisects the long rows of offices. Like the exterior of the building, the side walls of the hall are surfaced with a local hard-pressed red brick, its non-structural character expressed by continuous joints. Glass closes the two ends, but the brick walls

and plaster ceiling run out beyond to suggest indefinitely prolonged space. The rear view is the more attractive, as it is without the pretentious double-forked ramp which leads up to the front of the building.

The structure is reinforced concrete, with flat slab floors, and is completely air-conditioned. Office windows are arranged in an uninterrupted band behind the columns for even, glareless light. The plywood partitions were installed after completion of the continuous floor and ceiling, and can easily be moved to meet changing space requirements.

The heavy symmetry of the building is an anachronism partially justified by the fact that modern architects have not yet developed any popularly intelligible substitute for traditional forms of monumentality.

A city hall has a social importance which must somehow be symbolized.

Entrance canopy.

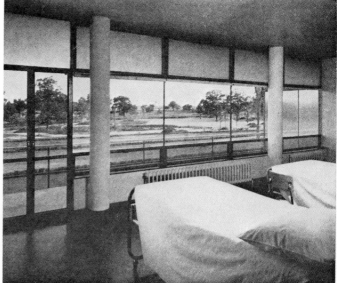

Typical bedroom.

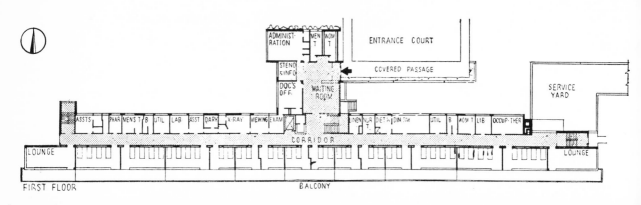

FIRST FLOOR

ADMINISTRATION · MEN T · WOM T · ENTRANCE COURT · STENO & INFO · COVERED PASSAGE · DOC'S OFF · WAITING ROOM · SERVICE YARD · ASSTS · PHAR · MEN S T B · UTIL · LAB · ASST · DARK · X-RAY · VIEWING · EXAM · LINEN · NUR DIET T · DIN RM · UTIL B · WOM T · LIB · OCCUP·THER · CORRIDOR · LOUNGE · LOUNGE · BALCONY

William A. Ganster and William L. Pereira: Lake County Tuberculosis Sanatorium, Waukegan, Illinois. 1939

Tubercular patients need sunny, quiet, uncluttered rooms which open widely to broad sheltered terraces—requirements incompatible with "Georgian" façades. Here the complicated demands of the modern sanatorium have been realistically analyzed and cleanly met, although one may question the absence of shelter over the upper balcony.

Most of the bedrooms are on the quieter side of the handsome reinforced concrete building, arranged on two floors in long south-facing rows for a maximum of sun. Each faces its balcony with a wall of glass: frosted glass at the top to reduce glare, then clear glass for the view and ventilating transoms below. Beds can be rolled onto the terrace through the broad doors.

Main entrance, administrative offices and out-patients' clinic are grouped in the north wing.

The continuous cantilevered roof trusses of the Assembly Plant.

Below: Shipping platforms with Export Building at right.

Albert Kahn Associated Architects & Engineers, Inc.: Dodge Half-Ton Truck Plant, Mound Road, Detroit, Michigan. 1938

American factories have long been famous for size and for efficiency of plan and structure, but too often their straightforward design is ruined by incongruous ornamental detail, or by a heavy and symmetrical block of administrative offices.

This quarter-mile long plant is throughout as unaffected in appearance as the handsome Export Building (above and at left) which is a slightly separated structure. Its supporting skeleton is steel, partly welded, partly riveted, and the unusual relationship between columns, supporting girders, roof trusses and clearstory is expressed in the façade. Enclosing walls are of brick and glass, surmounted by a thin band of sprayed concrete.

A row of ten such units, their long sides opened to each other, constitute the main body of the adjacent Assembly Plant. Here the roof trusses are cantilevered from one unit to the next (top left) for a maximum of open floor space.

Mies van der Rohe, architect; Holabird & Root, associated architects: Metallurgical Research Building of Armour Research Foundation, Illinois Institute of Technology, Chicago, Illinois. 1943

A shell of steel, and brick and glass, planned to house a great variety of industrial research activities. The central part is open through all three floors for utmost flexibility.

The function and form of each element has been so carefully studied and the relationship between materials so delicately adjusted, that the resulting structure is superbly well integrated, technically and esthetically, perhaps to the critical point of over-refinement.

The position of each small buff brick has been precisely calculated, door openings are subtly related to the total design, and the glass surfaces are so designed that the frames of fixed and movable panes are uniformly dimensioned. The exposed steel frame is painted black.

The perfection of detail is illustrated by the horizontal sections below: A shows the relationship between brick, steel and glass at the corner of an upper floor; B is the same corner close to the ground; C shows the box column, composed of two channels, at the center of the end wall and D is the wider column at its left.

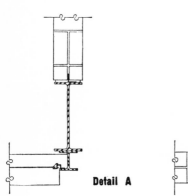

Detail A

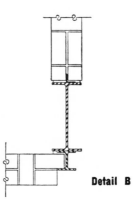

Detail B

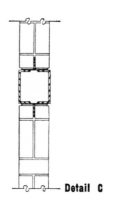

Detail C

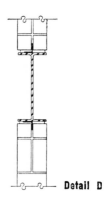

Detail D

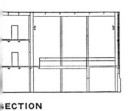

SECTION

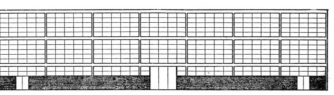

FRONT

SIDE

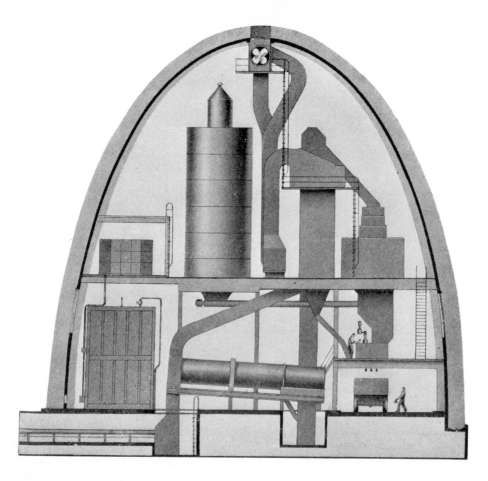

Light steel trusses served as reinforcement

Interior of the main conveyor tube

Municipal Asphalt Plant, East River Drive and 91st Street, New York, N. Y. Designed by the Department of Borough Works of the Office of the Borough President of Manhattan. Exterior architectural design by Ely Jacques Kahn and Robert Allan Jacobs. 1944

Sharply diversified industrial operations invite sharply differentiated architectural forms. Here there are three distinct and well related elements: conveyor belt, storage building and mixing plant. The main conveyor belt starts by the East River barge moorings, runs under the Drive, then above ground through a diagonal tube (later to be cased in chromium) to the rectangular storage building, where the sand and stone is dropped into a network of bins. From there underground conveyors run to the third and most prominent unit, the mixing plant.

The bold semi-ellipse of the mixing plant is no affectation. As the diagram shows, these clean curves represent the most efficient structural form which could house the machinery. The building is of reinforced concrete, its thin vault strengthened by 90-foot-high ribs. Since the ribs are reinforced with self-supporting steel trusses rather than with rods, no elaborate scaffolding was required.

Here is industrial architecture which is a distinct asset to its residential neighborhood and an exciting experience for motorists on the adjacent super-highway.

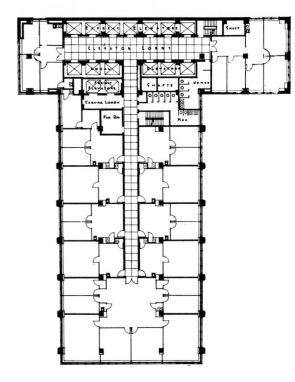

The banking room is on the second floor, quickly accessible by escalator. Shops are beneath. The room itself is handsome, but the exterior of the three lower stories, dark granite and glass, is indecisive in its relation to the rest of the design. The entire building is air-conditioned.

George Howe and William Lescaze: Philadelphia Saving Fund Society Building, Market Street at 12th, Philadelphia, Pennsylvania. 1932

Built by the oldest bank in the United States, the PSFS is a dramatic expression of the steel skeleton and the many identical floors of the modern office building.

Above the fifth floor the building assumes its characteristic T-shape. The typical plan shows how elevators and ducts are concentrated in one smooth block of glazed black brick. Offices project in a narrow wing for favorable light, with columns revealed on either side as vertical shafts. At the front, floors are cantilevered beyond the columns to allow continuous glass for maximum light and freedom of interior arrangement. Between the bands of glass are bands of light gray brick.

Rockefeller Center, New York, N. Y. Reinhard & Hofmeister, Corbett, Harrison & MacMurray, Hood & Fouilhoux, architects. 1932-1940

The only group of skyscrapers to be planned as a unit, Rockefeller Center shows the advantages of central control of land use, even when it is the control by a private corporation of the relatively small area of twelve acres.

The taller buildings are well separated. Their thin cross-sections and the staggered layout of the group insure each office a maximum of light and air. The interplay of their attenuated slab-like forms as one sees them from changing angles is one of the exciting urban experiences of our time.

With the exception of the new Eastern Airlines Building (stairway shown above), the individual buildings have little architectural distinction. But the bold conception and convincing urbanity of the whole have captured the public's imagination and Rockefeller Center has become not only a business center, but a civic monument.

If the profiles of the earlier skyscrapers were less blurred with "set-backs" and superfluous ornament and the ground less cluttered with minor, often symmetrically disposed structures, the result would rival the Pyramids in geometric splendor.

William Wilson Wurster: Office Building for the Schuckl Canning Company, Sunnyvale, California. 1942

A small rural office building in which the peculiar conditions of restricted materials, isolated site and warm climate have been met in a solution of notable elegance. Half of the ground floor is devoted to offices for local operations, the remainder opened as sheltered parking space. Above are the executive offices, moved from San Francisco, and on the roof are cafeteria and outdoor recreation deck for the use of employees.

The building is of wood, a non-priority material at the time of construction, and the decisively horizontal window strips are alternated with bands of brown-stained vertical boarding. On the south the glass is protected from the high summer sun by continuous coral-painted wooden sunblinds.

105

The building as seen from the service drive.

Pietro Belluschi: Shopping Center for FPHA war housing, McLoughlin Heights, Vancouver, Washington. 1942

Concentrated in one group are all the shops which serve the 4,500 families of a large war housing project. Parking space has been carefully planned in relation to the building, and separated from the service drive.

The shops enclose a landscaped court, and the covered passages make excellent sense in the rainy climate of the Northwest. Clearstory windows are inserted into the sloping roof. The wood frame is covered with vertical pine boards, unpainted but darkened with a protective coat of oil, and doors are red.

Shopping is sociable, and this building has all the appropriate lightness and gaiety.

The original plans included a theatre, a beer hall, bowling alleys and other recreational facilities, but these could not be built under wartime restrictions. Ideally, such a center would also contain a children's play-yard for the convenience of shopping mothers, and would be related by a system of traffic-free footpaths to every house in the community.

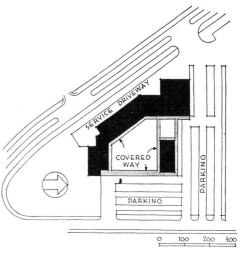

Raphael S. Soriano: Garden Center for the Hallawell Seed Company, 19th Avenue at Sloat Boulevard, San Francisco, California. 1942

A subtle and gaily persuasive setting for the sale of seeds and plants and flowers. Light and shade have been as skilfully composed as steel and glass and cement.

The building stretches along the highway for more than a hundred feet. Silhouetted against a grove of eucalyptus trees, its long sweep of roof seems suspended above the deep shadows and brightly emerging colors below.

The "lath house" is a popular California device for protecting young plants from excessive sunlight. Its latticed roof casts a shifting pattern of sun and shadow. On the west and south, screen walls of blue plate glass serve as windbreaks. The light steel skeleton which supports the roof is painted Chinese red.

A staggered row of wooden lath-roofed plant bars suggests a boundary to the ell-shaped court formed by store and lath house.

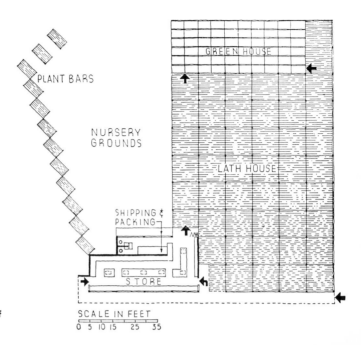

PLANT BARS

NURSERY GROUNDS

GREEN HOUSE

LATH HOUSE

SHIPPING & PACKING

STORE

SCALE IN FEET
0 5 10 15   25   35

Below: View to store from lath house, with latticed roof reflected in the blue plate glass at left.

Key: 1, entrance from West Boulevard; 2, truck entrance; 3, ramp to roof parking; 4, main sales building; 5, service building; 6, outdoor sales pavilion; 7, service station.

John Stokes Redden, architect; John Gerard Raben, designer: Retail Store for Sears Roebuck and Company, Pico Boulevard, Los Angeles, California. 1939

A suburban store adapted to the special needs of its motoring customers through the utilization of parking areas at various levels, connected by ramps. The lively arrangement of horizontal planes has an esthetic interest even beyond its practical advantages. More decisive, better-placed lettering would have contributed to the success of the design.

From the roof, stairs and escalator lead down to the windowless main sales building. From the lower parking lot one can enter the store directly or climb to the long balcony off the second floor.

Tennessee Valley Authority and Bureau of Reclamation: Storage Dam and Powerhouse, Norris, Tennessee. 1936

No gesture has been wasted. The bold diagonals of the huge dam, the sober rectangles of the reinforced concrete powerhouse and the finely etched lines of the transformers combine to form one of the monuments of our civilization.

Architects were for too long dreamily content with the application of "tasteful" superficial ornament to the daring construction of the engineers. Sometimes their decoration grew so bold that it swallowed up and denied the structure beneath. Almost any skyscraper is evidence.

Modern architecture has brought a new set of values, dependent for their realization upon the complete collaboration of architect and engineer. There is no better example than the work of the Tennessee Valley Authority and this early group at Norris.

Tennessee Valley Authority: Watts Bar Steam Plant, near Dayton, Tennessee. 1942

The conveyor carries coal to the larger section of the building (90 feet high from ground to roof coping), where it is pulverized and blown into the furnaces. Since glass would require continuous and hopeless washing under these circumstances, windows are almost entirely replaced by air-intake openings, and it is these long horizontal slits, protected by sheet metal hoods, which give this part of the building its striking appearance.

The lower block contains the steam-electric generators. Here abundant natural light was possible and desirable, as operations are both clean and exacting. Since ventilation is mechanical, insulating glass block could be used as a continuous strip beneath the roof.

The building's steel skeleton is covered outside with buff brick, and the great smoke stacks are black. Typical of TVA thoroughness is the excellent design of street lights and conveyor.

Belt Parkway Footbridge, Shore Parkway & Bay 46th Street, Brooklyn, New York. Designed by Clarence C. Combs, landscape architect for New York City Parks Department. 1939

Pedestrian Passerelle, North Avenue & Lake Shore Drive, Lincoln Park, Chicago, Illinois. Designed by the Engineering Division of the Chicago Park District: Ralph H. Burk, chief engineer. 1940

Through its singleness of purpose, made visible in daring, economical structure and unified form, a bridge can achieve a spare and muscular beauty which is unique. There is no one fine formula. The designer must to a great extent *choose* his conditions and his forms. There is not only the choice of location, of material, of general structural principle and its specific and harmonious development, but there is the choice of detail—railings, lights, approaches, etc., which can either affirm or negate the clean economy of the essential form. There are many paths to error.

Even that great suspension bridge, the Bronx-Whitestone, is not wholly satisfactory. The arches of its steel supports are, for example, quite arbitrarily reminiscent of masonry construction. Yet the bridge has a weightless grace which fairly sings.

The steel spans of the footbridges are buttressed with reinforced concrete, which, in the Chicago example, becomes cantilevered access ramps.

Opposite: Bronx-Whitestone Bridge, Eastern Boulevard (E 177 St.), New York, N. Y. For the Triborough Bridge Authority: O. H. Ammann, chief engineer; Allston Dana, engineer of design; Aymar Embury II, architect. 1939

BIOGRAPHICAL INDEX

CIRINO, Nicholas. Born 1907 in Matrice, Italy.

1930   B.Arch. University of California
1931   Graduate study, architecture and engineering
1932-35 California State Highway Department
1936   Los Angeles Bureau of Power and Light, Boulder Dam Transmission Line
1937   Planner's Representative, Resettlement Administration
1937-42 Regional Engineer, Farm Security Administration
1942-   District Engineer, Farm Security Administration
Woodville Farm Workers' Community, p.60
   *Pencil Points, Nov. '41, pp.709-20

COMBS, Clarence C.

Belt Parkway Footbridge, p.114

CORBETT, Harvey Wiley. Born 1873 in San Francisco, Calif.

1895   B.S. University of California
1900   Graduate in architecture, Ecole des Beaux Arts, Paris
1901-03 Office of Cass Gilbert, New York
1903-12 Partnership with F. Livingston Pel!
1912-22 Partnership with Frank J. Helmle
1915-25 Critic and lecturer, School of Architecture, Columbia University
1922-33 Partnership: Corbett, Harrison & MacMurray
1933   Chairman of Architectural Commission, 1933 Chicago World's Fair
1933-41 Partnership: Corbett and MacMurray
1935-   Member, Board of Directors, Regional Plan Association
1941-   Independent practice
Rockefeller Center, p.102
   *Giedion, Sigfried: Space, Time and Architecture, pp.569-80

DAILEY, Gardner A. Born 1895 in St. Paul, Minn.

1916   Traveled in Central America
1919   Studied at University of California
        Assistant engineer, Sonora Development Co., Mexico
1920   Stanford University
1921-22 Heals Engineering School, San Francisco
1926   Traveled in Europe and North Africa
1926   Established own office in San Francisco
1937   Traveled in Europe
1937   House and Garden Competition, second prize
        House Beautiful Competitions: first prizes, 1936, 1937, 1940; regional prize, 1941
1943   In Brazil: Chief Architect-Engineer for Amazon Division of the Rubber Development Corporation
1944-   President, San Francisco Planning Commission
Owens House, p.32
   *Arch. Forum, May '41, pp.363-65
U.S. Merchant Marine Cadet Basic School, p.78
   *Arch. Forum, Sept. '43, pp.55-9

DANA, Allston

Bronx-Whitestone Bridge, p.115
   *Arch. Forum, Sept. '39, pp.146-8

DeMARS, Vernon. Born 1908 in San Francisco, Calif.

1931   B.Arch. University of California
1932-37 Experience in San Francisco offices; private practice and work with Resettlement Administration
1937-39 Worked with Burton D. Cairns in Resettlement Administration (later Farm Security Administration) on housing projects for the Southwestern States

1938   Studied housing and city planning in Europe
1939-43 Chief Architect, Pacific Coast Region, Farm Security Administration
1943-   Chief, Housing Standards Section, National Housing Agency
Chandler Farm Workers' Community, p.62
   *Arch. Forum, Jan. '41, pp.8-11
   *Roth, Alfred: The New Architecture, pp.61-70
Woodville Farm Workers' Community, p.60
   *Pencil Points, Nov. '41, pp.709-20

DOYLE, A. E. See also BELLUSCHI, Pietro

Watzek House, p.40
   *Arch. Forum, Dec. '40, pp.56-8

EMBURY, Aymar, II

Bronx-Whitestone Bridge, p.115
   *Arch. Forum, Sept. '39, pp.146-8

FARM SECURITY ADMINISTRATION

Chandler Farm Workers' Community, p.62
   *Arch. Forum, Jan. '41. pp.8-11
   *Roth, Alfred: The New Architecture, pp.61-70
Woodville Farm Workers' Community, p.60
   *Pencil Points, Nov. '41, pp.709-20

FOUILHOUX, J. André. Born 1879 in Paris, France.

1898   B.A., B.S. and B.Ph. degrees, Sorbonne
1901   Received civil and mechanical engineering degree Ecole Centrale des Arts et Manufactures
1908-17 Partnership: Whitehouse & Fouilhoux, Portland, Ore.
1919   Office of Albert Kahn, Detroit
1920-34 Partnership: Hood, Godley & Fouilhoux
1935-41 Partnership: Harrison & Fouilhoux
1941-   Partnership: Harrison, Fouilhoux & Abramovitz
        Visiting critic, School of Architecture, Columbia University
Rockefeller Center, p.102
   *Giedion, Sigfried: Space, Time and Architecture, pp.569-80

FRANKLIN, Charles H. Born 1891 in San Francisco, Calif.

        Studied architecture and structural engineering for six years in the office of Reid Brothers, Architects, San Francisco. Passed California State examinations in 1917
1917-32 Partnership: Felchlin, Shaw & Franklin, Fresno, Calif.
1932-35 Own office, Fresno
1935-42 Partnership with Ernest J. Kump
1942-   Major, Corps of Engineers, U. S. Army
Acalanes Union High School, p.76
   *Arch. Record, June '41, pp.82-7
Fresno City Hall, p.90
   *Arch. Forum, June '44

FUNK, John. Born 1908 in Upland, Calif.

1934   B.Arch. University of California
1935   M.Arch. University of California
1936-38 Office of William Wilson Wurster
1938   Traveled in Europe
1939   Established own office, San Francisco
Heckendorf House, p.30
   *Arch. Forum, Mar. '41, pp.194-6

GANSTER, William A. Born 1908 in Evanston, Ill.

1930	B.S.Arch. University of Illinois
1930–37	Staff, Department of Architecture, University of Illinois
1935	M.S.Arch. University of Illinois
1937–42	Private practice, Waukegan, Ill.
1942–	Architect, Navy Department of Public Works, Great Lakes, Ill.

Lake County Tuberculosis Sanatorium, p.92
   *Arch. Forum, Sept. '40, pp.146–57

GOODWIN, Philip Lippincott. Born 1885 in New York City.

1907	B.A. Yale University
1909–12	Columbia School of Architecture
1912–14	Studied architecture in Paris
1914–16	Office of Delano & Aldrich
1916–21	Partnership: Goodwin, Bullard & Woolsey
1921	Established own office in New York
1935–	Chairman, Architecture Committee, Museum of Modern Art
1939	Festival Theatre, College of William and Mary Competition, with Edward D. Stone, second and third prizes
	Smithsonian Gallery of Art Competition, with Albert Frey and L. C. Jaeger, one of eight third prizes
1942	Trip to Brazil
1942–	Chairman, Committee on Foreign Affairs, American Institute of Architects
1943	Author: Brazil Builds

Museum of Modern Art, p.88
   *Arch. Forum, Aug. '39, pp.115–28

GROPIUS, Walter. Born 1883 in Berlin, Germany.

1904–07	Studied architecture at the Berlin and Munich Technical Institutes
1907–08	Traveled in Spain, Italy and England
1908–10	Assistant to Peter Behrens
1910–14	Own office, Berlin
1914	Director of the Industrial Section of the Werkbund Exposition, Cologne
1918	Founded the Arbeitsrat für Kunst
1919	Appointed Director of the Grand Ducal Art School and Arts and Crafts School at Weimar which he united and reorganized under the name of the Staatliches Bauhaus
1925	Bauhaus moved to Dessau
1928	Resumed private practice in Berlin
	Won first prize in Federal Government competition for the experimental Siedlung at Berlin-Haselhorst, and also in the competition for the Dammerstock Siedlung at Karlsruhe
1929	Received degree of Honorary Doctor from the Technical Institute, Hanover
1930	Directed the Deutscher Werkbund Exhibition at Paris Salon
	Chairman, Committee on Design, Adler Automobile Company
1931	Vice-President, International Congress Modern Architecture (C.I.A.M.)
1934	To London
1936–37	Partnership with Maxwell Fry, London
1937–	Professor, Department of Architecture, Harvard University. Later Chairman of Department
1937–40	Partnership with Marcel Breuer
1938	Competition for a New Art Center at Wheaton College, with Marcel Breuer, second prize
1942	Honorary M.A. degree from Harvard University

Chamberlain House, p.36
   *Arch. Forum, Nov. '42, pp.76–7
Ford House, p.38
   *Arch. Record, Mar. '40, pp.108–11

HARRIS, Harwell Hamilton. Born 1903 in Redlands, Calif.

	Attended Pomona College and Otis Art Institute. Studied engineering with M. T. Cantell and town planning with Richard J. Neutra
1930–33	Collaborated with Neutra on C.I.A.M. projects.
1931–33	Secretary, American Group, C.I.A.M.
1934	Own Office, Los Angeles
	Taught at Chouinard Art School and Art Center School, Los Angeles. Visiting critic, University of Southern California, University of California at Los Angeles, and Columbia University
	Pittsburgh Glass Institute awards—two first prizes
	House Beautiful awards—two mentions
1943–	In New York

House in Fellowship Park, p.34
   *Arch. Forum, Apr. '37, pp.278–81

HARRISON, Wallace Kirkman. Born 1895 in Worcester, Mass.

	Studied at Ecole des Beaux Arts, Paris
	Rotch Traveling Fellowship
1927–35	Partnership: Corbett, Harrison & MacMurray
1935–41	Partnership with J. André Fouilhoux
	Professor of Design, Columbia University
	Associate Professor of Design, Yale University
1941–	Partnership: Harrison, Fouilhoux & Abramovitz
1941–43	Assistant Coordinator of Inter-American Affairs
1943–	Consultant to Coordinator of Inter-American Affairs

Rockefeller Center, p.102
   *Giedion, Sigfried: Space, Time and Architecture, pp.569–80

HOFMEISTER, Henry. Born 1890 in New York City.

	Studied at Hornbostel Atelier and Beaux Arts Institute of Design, New York
1912	Worked in Rio de Janeiro for New York architectural firm
1925–28	With Todd, Robertson & Todd, New York
1928–	Partnership with L. Andrew Reinhard
	Pittsburgh Glass Competition awards, with L. Andrew Reinhard, 1937, 1938

Rockefeller Center, p.102
   *Giedion, Sigfried: Space, Time and Architecture, pp.569–80

HOOD, Raymond M. Born 1881 in Pawtucket, R. I. Died 1934.

1903	B.S. Massachusetts Institute of Technology
1911	Graduate in architecture, Ecole des Beaux Arts, Paris
	Worked in the offices of Cram, Goodhue & Ferguson, Boston; Palmer, Hornbostel & Jones, New York; Henry Hornbostel, Pittsburgh. Later established own office
1922	International competition for Chicago Tribune Tower, with John Mead Howells, first prize
1927–31	Partnership: Hood, Godley & Fouilhoux

1931–34	Partnership: Hood & Fouilhoux
1931	Honorary M.A. degree from Brown University
1932–34	Associated architect for Rockefeller Center
1933	Associated architect for Century of Progress Fair, Chicago

Rockefeller Center, p.102

*Giedion, Sigfried: *Space, Time and Architecture*, pp.569–80

HORSLEY, S. Clements. Born 1894 in Brigham City, Utah.

Studied at Brigham Young University, University of Utah, University of California. Graduate work at University of Pennsylvania. Study and travel in Europe.

1921–29	Offices of Samuel Yellin; Mellor, Meigs & Howe; Charles Klauder; Voorhees, Gmelin & Walker
1929–35	Private practice in New York
	Architectural League Prefabrication Competition, first prize
1935–38	Chief, Architectural Section, "Special Plans," Resettlement Administration
1938–	Private practice, New York

Johnson House, p.46

*Arch. Forum, Dec. '43, pp.89–93

HOWE, George. Born 1886 in Worcester, Mass.

1908	A.B. Harvard University
1912	Graduate in architecture, Ecole des Beaux Arts, Paris
1913–28	Partnership with Walter Mellor and Arthur I. Meigs, Philadelphia
1929–33	Partnership with William Lescaze
1933–	Private practice in Philadelphia
1941	Partnership with Louis I. Kahn
1942	Partnership: Howe, Stonorov, and Kahn
1942–	Supervising Architect, Public Buildings Administration, Federal Works Agency

Carver Court, p.66

Philadelphia Saving Fund Society, p.100

*Arch. Forum, Dec. '32, pp.482–98, 543–6

Thomas House, p.44

*Arch. Forum, Dec. '39, pp.447–54

HOYT, Burnham. Born 1887 in Denver, Col.

Studied at the Beaux-Arts Institute of Design, New York

Office of George B. Post & Sons, seven years

Office of Bertram Goodhue, two years

1919–23	Partnership with his brother, M. H. Hoyt, Denver
1926	Came to New York to design Riverside Church
	Office of Pelton, Allen & Collens, six years
1929–33	Taught design at New York University, School of Architecture
1933–	Private practice, Denver

Red Rocks Amphitheatre, p.87

JACKSON, Huson. Born 1913 in Sewickley, Pa.

1934	Ph.B. University of Chicago
1935–36	Office of Charles Eames and Robert Walsh, St. Louis
1938	B.Arch. Harvard University
1939	M.Arch. Harvard University
1939–40	United States Housing Authority
1940	Office of Hilyard R. Robinson, Washington, D. C.
1940–42	Associated with Joseph P. Richardson and Carl Koch, Boston

1942–44	Architect for Aluminum Ore Company and practice in St. Louis

Group of Houses, Snake Hill, p.54

JACOBS, Robert Allan. Born 1905 in New York City.

1927	B.A. Amherst College
1934	B.Arch. Columbia University
1934–35	Office of Le Corbusier, Paris
1935	Interpreter for Le Corbusier during his three month lecture tour of the U. S.
1935–38	Office of Harrison & Fouilhoux
1938–40	Office of Ely Jacques Kahn
1940–	Firm of Ely Jacques Kahn and Robert Allan Jacobs

Municipal Asphalt Plant, p.98

*Arch. Forum, Mar. '44, pp.109–12

JOHNSON, Philip. Born 1906 in Cleveland, Ohio.

1932–34	Chairman, Department of Architecture, Museum of Modern Art
1932	Co-author with Henry-Russell Hitchcock, Jr.: *The International Style: Architecture since 1922*
1943	B.Arch. Harvard University
1943–	U. S. Army Engineer Corps

Johnson House, p.46

*Arch. Forum, Dec. '43, pp.89–93

JOHNSON, Reginald Davis. Born 1882 in Westchester, New York.

1907	B.A. Williams College
1910	B.S. Massachusetts Institute of Technology
	Extensive residential and public housing work
1911–	Own office, Los Angeles

Baldwin Hills Village, p.56

KAHN, Albert. Born 1869, Westphalia, Germany. Died 1942.

1881	Came to U. S.
	Office of George D. Mason, Detroit, for fourteen years
1890	Won *American Architect* scholarship for study abroad
1896–'42	Office, Albert Kahn Inc., Detroit
1917	Official architect for Aircraft Construction Division, Signal Corps, U.S. Army
1928–31	Factories for Russia's first five-year plan
1942	Awarded honorary degree, Doctor of Fine Arts, by Syracuse University

Dodge Half-Ton Truck Plant, p.94

*Nelson, George: *Industrial Architecture of Albert Kahn Inc.*

*Arch. Record, June '39, pp.110–15

KAHN, Ely Jacques. Born 1884 in New York City.

1903	B.A. Columbia University
1907	B.Arch. Columbia University
1911	Graduate in architecture, Ecole des Beaux Arts, Paris
1915	Professor of Design, Cornell University
1917–30	Partnership: Buckman & Kahn
1930–40	Own office, New York
1932	Instructor of Design, New York University
1934	Grant from Carnegie Corporation
1935	Author of *Design in Art and Industry*
1940–	Firm of Ely Jacques Kahn and Robert Allan Jacobs

Municipal Asphalt Plant, p.98

*Arch. Forum, Mar. '44, pp.109–12

KAHN, Louis I. Born 1901, Island of Ösel, Russia.

	Studied at Public Industrial Art School, Philadelphia
	Graduated from University of Pennsylvania
1926	Chief of Design for Philadelphia Sesqui-Centennial Exposition
	Studied and traveled in Europe
1931	Began Architects' Research Group, Philadelphia, to study city planning problems
1934	In charge of housing studies, Philadelphia City Planning Commission
1935-42	Private practice, Philadelphia
1938	Consultant to Philadelphia Housing Authority
1939	Consultant to U.S. Housing Authority
1941	Partnership with George Howe
1942	Partnership: Howe, Stonorov, and Kahn
1942-	Partnership with Oscar Stonorov
1943	Co-author with Oscar Stonorov of pamphlet: *Why City Planning is Your Responsibility*

Carver Court, p.66

KENNEDY, Robert.

Group of Houses, Snake Hill, p.54

KLING, Vincent G. Born 1916 in East Orange, N. J.

1938	B.A. Columbia University
1940	B.Arch. Columbia University
1941-	U.S. Navy, now Lieutenant (j.g.)
1942	M.Arch. Massachusetts Institute of Technology

Peaslee House, p.48
  *Arch. Forum, Mar. '42, pp.188-92

KOCH, Carl. Born 1912 in Milwaukee, Wis.

1934	B.A. Harvard University
1937	M.Arch. Harvard University
1937-42	Private practice. Also worked temporarily in the offices of Edward D. Stone; Sven Markelius, Stockholm; Gropius & Breuer
1938-39	Bacon Traveling Fellowship
1938	Pittsburgh Glass Competition, with Edward D. Stone, first prize
1939	*House and Garden* Competition, with Edward D. Stone, first prize
1941	Organic Design Competition, furniture for a dining room, honorable mention
1941-42	National Advisory Committee on Design, United States Housing Authority
1942-	Director, Planning and Building Associates
1942-44	Senior Research Technician, Standards Section, National Housing Agency
1944-	U.S. Navy, Lt. (j.g.)

Group of Houses, Snake Hill, p.54
  *Arch. Forum, June '41, pp.382-93 (first five houses)

KUMP, Ernest J. Born 1911 in Bakersfield, Calif.

1932	B.Arch. University of California
1932-33	Office of Ernest J. Kump, Sr.
1934	M.Arch. Harvard University
1934-42	Partnership with Charles H. Franklin, Fresno
1937-	National Advisory Council on School Building Problems, U.S. Office of Education
1942-	Ernest J. Kump Co., San Francisco

Acalanes Union High School, p.76
  *Arch. Record, June '41, pp.82-7
Fresno City Hall, p.90
  *Arch. Forum, June '44

LESCAZE, William. Born 1896 in Geneva, Switzerland.

	M.Arch. Federal Polytechnical Institute, Zurich
1920	Came to U.S.
1923-29	Own office, New York
1929-34	Partnership with George Howe, New York
1934-	Own office, New York
	Technical adviser, State of New York, Division of Housing
1935	Author: *Architecture for the New Theatre*
1941	Author: *The Intent of the Artist*
1942	Author: *On Being an Architect*

Norman House, p.50
Philadelphia Saving Fund Society, p.100
  *Arch. Forum, Dec. '32, pp.482-98,543-6

MacMURRAY, W. H. 1868-1941

Rockefeller Center, p.102

MANHATTAN DEPARTMENT OF BOROUGH WORKS

Municipal Asphalt Plant, p.98
  *Arch. Forum, Mar. '44, pp.109-12

MERRILL, Edwin Ellison. Born 1890 in Albany, Oregon.

1913	B.S. University of California
1915	B.S. Massachusetts Institute of Technology
1915-23	Worked in architectural offices and with the U.S. Navy
1924-36	Partnership with Lewis Eugene Wilson
1936-42	Partnership: Wilson, Merrill & Alexander
1942-	Partnership: Wilson & Merrill

Baldwin Hills Village, p.56

MERRILL, John O. Born 1896 in St. Paul, Minn.

1921	B.S.Arch. Massachusetts Institute of Technology
1921-26	Office of Lowe & Bollenbacher
1926-39	Partner of Grainger & Bollenbacher
1934-39	Chief Architect for FHA, Middlewestern States
1939-	Partnership: Skidmore, Owings and Merrill

Main Reception Building, p.80
  *Arch. Forum, Mar. '43, pp.55-60

MIES VAN DER ROHE, Ludwig. Born 1886 in Aachen, Germany.

1905-07	Furniture design, office of Bruno Paul, Berlin
1908-11	Assistant to Peter Behrens, Berlin
1911-38	Own office, Berlin
1926	First vice-president, Deutscher Werkbund
1927	Director, Werkbund Exposition, Stuttgart
	First sprung steel chair
1929	Director of German section, International Exposition, Barcelona
1930-33	Head of the Bauhaus, Dessau
1931	Director of Contemporary Dwelling section, Berlin Building Exposition
1933	Reichsbank Building Competition prize
1934	Architect for German section, International Exhibition, Brussels, Belgium
1934	Architect for Mining Industry Exhibit, Berlin Exhibition

1938–   Director and Professor, Department of Architecture,
         Armour Institute of Technology, Chicago
Metallurgical Research Building, p.96
   *Arch. Forum, Nov. '43, pp.88–90

NEUTRA, Richard J. Born 1892 in Vienna, Austria.

1909–12 Vienna Technical Institute
1912–14 Studied with Adolf Loos, Vienna
1919–20 Studied landscape architecture with Gustav Amman,
         Switzerland; also post-graduate work in architecture
         at Federal Polytechnic Institute
1921–22 Associated with Eric Mendelsohn, Berlin
1922   International Competition for business center at Jaffa,
         Palestine, with Eric Mendelsohn, first prize
1923–24 Came to U.S. Worked in architects' offices in New
         York and with Holabird & Root, Chicago
1925–   Own office, Los Angeles
1927   Author: Wie Baut Amerika? published in Stuttgart
1930   Author: Amerika. (Neues Bauen in der Welt, BD. II),
         published in Vienna
1930–31 Lecture tour: Japan, Europe, United States, Mexico
1933   Co-author: The Circle, London symposium
1935   House Beautiful Competition, first prize
         Better Homes in America, two first prizes
1941   Co-author: Preface to a Master Plan
         Consultant to National Youth Administration, United
         States Housing Authority, United States Treasury (on
         post office buildings), Federal Works Agency
         Member, National Advisory Council on School Building
         Problems, U.S. Office of Education
1941–43 California State Planning Board; chairman in 1943
1943–44 Lecturer on planning, Bennington College
1943–   Director of Design, Public Works Program, Insular
         Government of Puerto Rico
Channel Heights, p.68
   *Arch. Forum, Mar. '44, pp.65–74
Experimental School, p.72
   *Arch. Record, June '36, pp.453–6
   *Roth, Alfred: The New Architecture, pp.105–14

NEW YORK CITY PARKS DEPARTMENT
Belt Parkway Footbridge, p.114

OWINGS, N. A. Born 1903 in Indianapolis, Ind.

1927   B.A. Cornell University
         Traveled in Europe and Asia
1927–28 Worked in architects' offices, New York
1929   Partnership with Henry B. Crosby, New Jersey
1930–33 Development Supervisor in charge of production of
         architectural and engineering drawings and specifi-
         cations for A Century of Progress
1935–39 Partnership with Louis Skidmore
1939–   Partnership: Skidmore, Owings & Merrill
1943–   Member, City Planning Advisory Board, Chicago
1943–   Member, Blighted Areas Committee of Chicago Asso-
         ciation of Commerce
Main Reception Building, p.80
   *Arch. Forum, Mar. '43, pp.55–60

PEREIRA, William L. Born 1910 in Chicago, Ill.

         B.S.Arch. University of Illinois
1930–33 Office of Holabird & Root, Chicago

1933–   Own office
         In addition to architecture practice: Direction, Art
         Direction, Special Photography for Paramount Studios;
         Direction and Production Design for David O. Selznick
         Productions
Lake County Tuberculosis Sanatorium, p.92
   *Arch. Forum, Sept. '40, pp.146–57

PERKINS, Lawrence B. Born 1907 in Evanston, Ill.

1930   B.Arch. Cornell University
1931–33 Worked in architectural offices in Chicago
1933–34 Field experience as maintenance engineer for Arm-
         strong Paint and Varnish Works
1933–   With General Houses, Inc., Chicago
1935–36 Partnership with Philip Will, Jr.
1936–   Partnership: Perkins, Wheeler & Will
Crow Island School, p.74
   *Arch. Forum, Aug. '41, pp.79–92

RABEN, John Gerard
Sears Roebuck store, p.110
   *Arch. Forum, Feb. '40, pp.70–6

REDDEN, John Stokes
Sears Roebuck store, p.110
   *Arch. Forum, Feb. '40, pp.70–6

REINHARD, L. Andrew. Born 1891 in New York City.

         Studied at Mechanics' Institute and Columbia School of
         Architecture
1920–28 With Todd, Robertson & Todd, New York
1928–   Partnership with Henry Hofmeister
         Pittsburgh Glass Competition awards, with Henry
         Hofmeister, 1937, 1938
Rockefeller Center, p.102
   *Giedion, Sigfried: Space, Time and Architecture, pp.569–80

SAARINEN, Eero. Born 1910 in Kirkkonummi, Finland. Son of Eliel
Saarinen.

1923   Came to U.S.A.
1929–30 Studied sculpture at Académie de la Grande Chau-
         mière, Paris
1931–34 School of Architecture, Yale University
1934–35 Matcham Traveling Fellowship
1934   Post and Telegraph Building Competition for Helsinki,
         third prize
1935–36 Worked with Jarl Eklund in Helsinki
1936–38 City Planning and Housing Projects with Flint Institute
         of Research and Planning
1938–41 Associated with Eliel Saarinen
1939   Festival Theatre, College of William and Mary Com-
         petition, with Ralph Rapson and Fred James, first
         prize
         Smithsonian Gallery of Art Competition, Washington,
         D. C., with Eliel Saarinen and J. R. F. Swanson, first
         prize
1941   Organic Design Competition, with Charles Eames, seat-
         ing for a living room, first prize; other furniture for a
         living room, first prize
1941–   Partnership with Eliel Saarinen and J. R. F. Swanson
1942–   With Office of Strategic Services, Washington, D. C.

1943   *California Arts and Architecture* Competition, Design
        for Post War Living, with Oliver Lundquist, first prize
Crow Island School, p.74
    Arch. Forum, Aug. '41, pp.79–92

SAARINEN, Eliel. Born 1873 in Helsinki, Finland.
1897   Graduated from Polytechnical Institute of Helsinki
1897–'07 Partnership with Lindgren and Gesellius
1907–22 Own office in Helsinki. Extensive building and city
        planning practice. Won first prizes in seven national
        and two international competitions
1911   Planning consultant, Budapest, Hungary
1913   Planning consultant, Revel, Estonia
        Vice-president, International City Planning Confer-
        ences, for many years
1922   International Competition for Chicago Tribune Build-
        ing, second prize
1923   Came to U.S.A.
1924–25 Taught design, School of Architecture, University of
        Michigan
1925–   Architect for Cranbrook schools of art, Bloomfield
        Hills, Michigan. Now head of Cranbrook Academy of
        Art
1939   Smithsonian Gallery of Art Competition, Washington,
        D. C., with Eero Saarinen and J. R. F. Swanson, first
        prize
1941–   Partnership with Eero Saarinen and J. R. F. Swanson
1943   Author: *The City, Its Growth, Its Decline, Its Future*
        Honorary degrees from Technical University of Karls-
        ruhe, University of Finland, University of Michigan,
        Harvard University, Bethany College
Crow Island School, p.74
    Arch. Forum, Aug. '41, pp.79–92

SKIDMORE, Louis. Born 1897 in Lawrenceburg, Ind.
1920   Office of Kruckemeyer & Strong, Cincinnati
1921–24 Massachusetts Institute of Technology
1924–26 Office of Maginnis & Walsh, Boston
1926–29 Rotch Traveling Fellowship
1930–35 Assistant General Manager in Charge of Design and
        Construction, Century of Progress Fair, Chicago
1935–39 Partnership with N. A. Owings
1936   Consultant to Board of Design, New York World's Fair
1939–   Partnership: Skidmore, Owings & Merrill
Main Reception Building, p.80
    Arch. Forum, Mar. '43, pp.55–60

SORIANO, Raphael S. Born 1905, Island of Rhodes, Aegean Sea
1924   Came to U.S.A.
1932   Worked with Richard J. Neutra on planning project,
        Rush City Reformed
1934   B.Arch. University of Southern California
1935   Special projects for Regional Planning Commission.
        County of Los Angeles
1936–   Own office, Los Angeles
1940   American Gas Association Competition, honorable
        mention
1943   *California Arts and Architecture* Competition, Design
        for Post War Living, third prize
Hallawell Seed Company, p.108
    Arch. Forum, Aug. '43, pp.92–8

STEIN, Clarence S. Born 1882 in Rochester, N. Y.
1903–04 School of Architecture, Columbia University
1904–10 Studied at Ecole des Beaux Arts and traveled in
        Europe
1911–18 Office of Bertram G. Goodhue
1919–   Own office. Extensive practice in the planning and
        design of housing projects
1920   Secretary, Committee on Housing, New York State
        Reconstruction Commission
1923–26 Chairman, New York State Commission of Housing and
        Regional Planning
1924   Vice-President, International Garden Cities and Town
        Planning Federation
1924–29 Associated with Henry Wright on Sunnyside Gardens,
        Radburn, and Chatham Village
1925–37 Member, Executive Committee, International Federa-
        tion for Housing and Town Planning
Baldwin Hills Village, p.56

STONE, Edward D. Born 1902 in Fayetteville, Ark.
1919–23 University of Arkansas
1925–26 Studied architecture, Harvard University
1926–27 Studied architecture, M.I.T.
1927–29 Rotch Traveling Fellowship
1929–30 Office of Schultze & Weaver
1930–32 With Rockefeller Center Architects
1933–42 Independent practice
1934–35 Office of Wallace K. Harrison
1936–41 Instructor in Architectural Design, New York University.
        Member, Architectural Advisory Committee, Columbia
        University. Member, Architectural Advisory Committee,
        USHA
1938   Pittsburgh Glass Competition, grand prize
1939   *House and Garden* Competition, grand prize
        Festival Theatre, College of William and Mary Com-
        petition, with Philip L. Goodwin, second and third
        prizes
        Smithsonian Gallery of Art Competition, one of eight
        third prizes
1942–   Headquarters Army Air Forces, Washington, D. C.
        Now Major A. C.
Goodyear House, p.42
    Arch. Forum, July '41, pp.13–17
Museum of Modern Art, p.88
    Arch. Forum, Aug. '39, pp.115–28

STONOROV, Oscar. Born 1905 in Frankfurt-am-Main, Germany.
        Studied in Florence and under Karl Moser at Federal
        Polytechnic Institute, Zurich
        Studied sculpture with Aristide Maillol
        Office of André Lurçat, Paris
        Hospital building consultant to Mayor of Karlsruhe
1929   Trip to America
        Competition for National Theatre of the Ukraine,
        Krakow, fifth prize
1930   Collaborated with W. Boesiger in publication, *Le
        Corbusier und Pierre Jeanneret, Ihr Gesamtes Werk von
        1910–1929*
1932–35 Partnership with Alfred Kastner, New York
        Competition for the Palace of the Soviets, Moscow,
        with Alfred Kastner, second prize

1933	Helped organize National Labor Housing Conference
1941	Organic Design Competition, with Willo Von Moltke, furniture for a bedroom, first prize; seating for a living room, honorable mention
1942	Partnership: Howe, Stonorov and Kahn
1942–	Partnership with Louis I. Kahn
1943	Co-author with Louis I. Kahn of pamphlet, *Why City Planning is Your Responsibility*

Carver Court, p.66

STUBBINS, Hugh, Jr. Born 1912 in Birmingham, Ala.

1933	B.S.Arch. Georgia Tech
1935	M.Arch. Harvard University
1935–38	Designer, architectural office, Boston
1938–39	Partnership, Boston. Awards won with Marc Peter, Jr.: American Gas Competition, first prize; Competition for a Post Office and Court House, Covington, Kentucky, award; Festival Theatre, College of William and Mary Competition, fifth prize; Smithsonian Gallery of Art Competition, Washington, D. C., one of eight third prizes; Productive Home Competition, award; *Ladies' Home Journal—Architectural Forum* Competition, award
1939–	Instructor, Graduate School of Design, Harvard
1940–42	Private practice in Boston
1941	Organic Design Competition, furniture for a dining room, honorable mention
1941–42	Member, Architectural Advisory Committee, USHA

Windsor Locks, p.64
    Arch. Forum, May '42, pp.328–31

TENNESSEE VALLEY AUTHORITY

Norris Dam and Powerhouse, p.111
    Arch. Forum, Aug. '39, pp.81–3
Watts Bar Steam Plant, p.112

THOMSEN, Harry A., Jr. Born 1886 in San Francisco, Calif.

1906–10	Worked in San Francisco architectural offices
1908–12	Studied at San Francisco Architectural Club
1910–23	Office of George W. Kelham, San Francisco
1923–36	Partner of George W. Kelham
1936–	Own office, San Francisco

Valencia Gardens, p.58
    Pencil Points, Jan. '44, pp.26–36

TRIBOROUGH BRIDGE AUTHORITY

Bronx-Whitestone Bridge, p.115
    Arch. Forum, Sept. '39, pp.146–8

WHEELER, E. Todd. Born 1906 in Wilmette, Ill.

1929	B.S.Arch. University of Illinois
1929–35	Worked in architectural offices in Chicago
1935–36	With General Houses, Inc.
1936–	Partnership: Perkins, Wheeler & Will

Crow Island School, p.74
    Arch. Forum, Aug. '42, pp.79–92

WILL, Philip, Jr. Born 1906 in Rochester, N. Y.

1929	B.Arch. Cornell University
1930–33	Office of Shreve, Lamb and Harmon, New York
1933–35	With General Houses, Inc., Chicago

1935	With Associated Architects, South Park Gardens, Chicago
1935–36	Partnership with Lawrence B. Perkins
1936–	Partnership: Perkins, Wheeler & Will

Crow Island School, p.74
    Arch. Forum, Aug. '41, pp 79–92

WILSON, Lewis Eugene. Born 1900 in Excelsior Springs, Mo.

Worked in his father's office (George W. Wilson, Architect) through high school
Studied architecture at the University of Arkansas

1924–36	Partnership with Edwin Ellison Merrill
1934–36	Vice-president, Citizens' Housing Committee, Los Angeles
1936–42	Partnership: Wilson, Merrill & Alexander
1936–38	Vice-president, Los Angeles Housing Committee
1937–39	Vice-president, Metropolitan Housing Council, Los Angeles
1938–42	Extensive work in housing in association with various other architects
1942–	Partnership: Wilson & Merrill
1944–	President, Home Owners' League of America
1944	Consulting architect to Los Angeles Housing Authority

Baldwin Hills Village, p.56
Channel Heights, p.68
    Arch. Forum, Mar. '44, pp.65–74

WRIGHT, Frank Lloyd. Born 1869 in Richland Center, Wis.

1885–87	Studied engineering at the University of Wisconsin Building experience under Dean Conover
1887–88	Office of J. L. Silsbee, Chicago
1888–94	In charge of domestic building, office of Adler & Sullivan
1894–	Independent practice
1906	Trip to Japan
1910	Portfolio of his work published by Wasmuth, Berlin Trip to Germany and Italy
1916–20	Built Imperial Hotel, Tokyo
1930	Author: *Modern Architecture* (Kahn Lectures at Princeton University)
1932	Author: *The Disappearing City* and *An Autobiography*
1932	Foundation of the Taliesin Fellowship
1933–	Development of regional plan, Broadacre City
1937	Trip to U.S.S.R. Co-author with Baker Brownell, *Architecture and Modern Life*
1939	Trip to England Author: *An Organic Architecture: The Architecture of Democracy* (Sir George Watson lectures of Sulgrave Manor Board, London)
1943	Author: *An Autobiography* (revised and expanded version)
see also	*Frank Lloyd Wright on Architecture: Selected Writings, 1894–1940.* Edited with an introduction by Frederick Gutheim.

House at Bear Run, p.26
    Arch. Forum, Jan. '38, pp.36–47
    Henry-Russell Hitchcock, Jr.: In the Nature of Materials, illus. 320–23, 369–73
    A New House by Frank Lloyd Wright, Museum of Modern Art, 1938

Winkler-Goetsch House, p.28
  *Hitchcock: *In the Nature of Materials*, illus. 376–8
Taliesin West, p.84
  *Hitchcock: *In the Nature of Materials*, illus. 352–59

WURSTER, William Wilson. Born 1895 in Stockton, Calif.

1919	B.Arch. University of California
1920	Office of John Reid, Jr., San Francisco
1921–22	Associated with Charles F. Dean
1922–23	Travel in Europe
1923–24	Office of Delano & Aldrich, New York
1926–	Own office in San Francisco
	Competition awards from *House & Garden, Better Homes in America, House Beautiful*
1937	Travel in Europe, especially Scandinavia
1943–44	Fellowship for city and regional planning study, Harvard University
1943–44	Assistant Professor of Architectural Design, Yale University

Valencia Gardens, p.58
  Pencil Points, Jan '44, pp.26–36
Schuckl Office Building, p.104
  Arch. Forum, July '43, pp.110–15

YEON, John. Born 1910 in Portland, Ore.

	Technical training by apprenticeship in various architectural offices
1930	Traveled in Europe
1931–36	Worked on conservation, regional, state and city planning. Served on Oregon State Park Commission, Portland City Planning Commission, Oregon State Planning Board, Northwest Regional Planning Commission and Columbia Gorge Committee
1935–41	Private practice
1942–	Overseas with U. S. Engineers

Watzek House, p.40
  Arch. Record, Dec. '40, pp.56–8

ARCHITECTURAL EXHIBITIONS AND PUBLICATIONS
of the Museum of Modern Art

Exhibitions:

Years of original showing and circulation	Number of showings outside the museum	
		* not shown at the Museum.
		† specially prepared for circulation in collaboration with the Department of Circulating Exhibitions or, in some cases, with the Educational Program.
1932–34	14	Modern Architecture, International Exhibition.
		Virtually the first presentation of modern architecture to the American public and to American architects. The first Museum exhibition to travel to other cities. (See list of publications and page 9)
1932–38	17	Photographic Exhibition of Modern Architecture.*†
		A smaller edition of the first show.
1933	1	American Architecture Exhibition.
		Prepared for the Triennial Exhibition of Decorative Arts in Milan, Italy.
1933–36	6	Early Modern Architecture: Chicago 1870–1910.
		Pioneer research on the history of the skyscraper. The study was made in collaboration with Henry-Russell Hitchcock, Jr. (See list of publications.)
1933		The Work of Young Architects in the Middle West.
1933		Project for a House in North Carolina by W. T. Priestley.
1933		A House by Richard C. Wood.
1933	13	Walker Evans' Photographs of 19th Century Houses.
1934		The Philadelphia Saving Fund Society Building by Howe & Lescaze. (See page 100.)
1934		Early Museum Architecture.
1934		Housing Exhibition.
1934		America Can't Have Housing?
		This first important housing exhibition in the United States was prepared by a committee of experts with Carol Aronovici as chairman. (See list of publications.)
1935–39	20	Modern Architecture in California.
1935–38	14	Recent Work by Le Corbusier.
		Prepared to supplement lectures made by Le Corbusier in 21 cities, a tour arranged by the Department of Architecture.

Years of original showing and circulation	Number of showings outside the museum	
1936–40	14	Architecture of H. H. Richardson.
		Material collected by H.-R. Hitchcock, Jr., for his book. (See list of publications.)
1936–37	7	Cubism and Abstract Art (section on architecture).
1936		Architecture in Government Housing.
		The best of the work being produced under PWA and the Resettlement Administration.
1936–37	1	Modern Exposition Architecture.
1936–38	11	Fantastic Art, Dada and Surrealism (section on architecture).
1937–39	10	Modern Architecture in England.
		"This is the most serious and the most constructive evaluation of modern architecture in England that has yet been made."—*Journal of the Royal Institute of British Architects.* (See list of publications.)
1937		Project for a Community Center by the Architects', Painters' and Sculptors' Collaborative: Oscar Stonorov, Architect.
1937		Town of Tomorrow.
		A protest against the New York World's Fair project of that name.
1938–40	18	A New House by Frank Lloyd Wright on Bear Run, Pennsylvania. (See page 26.)
		(See list of publications.)
1938–41	15	Architecture and Furniture by Alvar and Aino Aalto.
		First American survey of the work of these important Finnish architects and furniture designers. (See list of publications.)
1938	1	Trois Siècles d'Art aux Etats-Unis* (section on architecture).
		Exhibition of American art from 1609–1938 prepared by the Museum and presented under the auspices of the French Government at the Musée du Jeu de Paume in Paris. (See list of publications.)
1938–41	17	Competition Designs for a New Art Center for Wheaton College.
		Results of a competition conducted by the Department of Architecture and the *Architectural Forum.*
1938–40	4	The Bauhaus: 1919–1928.
		A large exhibition, designed by Herbert Bayer, which illustrated the educational principles, aims and achievements of the first nine years of the famous German school. (See list of publications.)
1938–	71	What is Modern Architecture?†
		An exhibition of the problems and principles of the new architecture, prepared especially for schools and illustrated by examples of work here and abroad. Five editions made between 1938 and 1941, two for sale to other museums. (See list of publications.)
1938–41	24	Modern Houses in America.*†
1939–40	10	The Bauhaus: How it worked.*†
1939–41	11	Three Centuries of American Architecture.
		This domestic version of the architectural section of Trois Siècles d'Art aux Etats-Unis was a graphic revaluation of our architectural past. " . . . a very able and gratifying presentation of a subject that no one—I said no one—has yet fully encompassed in print." (Lewis Mumford in *The New Yorker,* March 11, 1939.)
1939–41	9	Competition Designs for a National Festival Theatre and Art Center at Williamsburg, Virginia.
1939–	10	Evolution of the Skyscraper.*†
		A small exhibition prepared to supplement the film of the same name.

Years of original showing and circulation	Number of showings outside the museum	
1939–40	6	Houses and Housing.
		The importance of good design in the modern dwelling, whether the single-family house, the apartment house or the large housing scheme. Prepared by the United States Housing Authority in Washington with the collaboration of the Department of Architecture and presented as a part of the Museum's Tenth Anniversary Exhibition. (See list of publications)
1939–43	9	Modern Interiors.†
		Specially designed for use in schools.
1939–40	3	Prize-Winning Designs for a New Smithsonian Gallery of Art.
1940–	30	A Survey of Housing in Europe and America.*†
1940–	20	Stockholm Builds.†
		Photographs by G. E. Kidder Smith of modern Swedish architecture.
1940–	21	The Wooden House in America.†
		An historical summary of our unique tradition of wood-building, with emphasis on modern examples.
1940		Twenty Centuries of Mexican Art (section on Mexican Colonial Architecture).
1941		Frank Lloyd Wright, American Architect.
		The first complete presentation. A catalog was planned, but not published. Some of the material was turned over to H.-R. Hitchcock, Jr., for his book on Wright's work, "In the Nature of Materials."
1941–42	5	T.V.A. Architecture and Design.
		Prepared by the Tennessee Valley Authority in collaboration with the Department of Architecture.
1941–	15	Regional Building in America.*†
		The influence of climate and locally available materials and techniques on the architecture of past and present.
1941–	19	American Architecture.*†
		A series of three small shows made up of revised sections of Three Centuries of American Architecture.
1942		Dymaxion Deployment Unit.
		Buckminster Fuller's round sheet-metal house, designed for mass fabrication, was erected in the Museum's garden.
1942	1	Architecture of Eric Mendelsohn: 1914–1940.
1942–	17	Planning the Modern House †
		A small show focused on a California house by John Funk (see page 30). Designed for the Educational Program by Elizabeth Mock (two copies).
1942–43	7	Wartime Housing.
		A timely and dramatic display of the crucial need for housing in war-expanded industrial areas. Prepared by the Departments of Architecture and Industrial Design with the advice of experts in the field.
1942–	13	Modern Architecture for the Modern School.†
		An exhibition based on the need of the elementary school child for psychologically congenial surroundings. Prepared by Elizabeth Mock for the Department of Circulating Exhibitions.
1943–	13	Brazil Builds: Architecture New and Old, 1652–1942.
		The exhibition was made up from material collected by Philip L. Goodwin for his book of the same title. Photographs by G. E. Kidder Smith. (See list of publications.) "It (Brazil Builds) makes known a whole new school of modern architecture . . . the only study to date of this remarkable achievement." (Robert C. Smith in the *Art News.)*
1943–	6	Brazil Builds.*†
		Four smaller versions of the above exhibition have been made: two for circulation in the United States, one for South America, one for England.

Years of original showing and circulation	Number of showings outside the museum	
1943		Five California Houses.
		Organized by Hervey Parke Clark, sponsored by *California Arts and Architecture,* and exhibited at the Museum after its original showing at the San Francisco Museum of Art.
1944–		Look at Your Neighborhood.†
		A multi-copy exhibition of neighborhood planning principles, prepared for the Department of Circulating Exhibitions by Rudolf Mock, with the advice of Clarence Stein.
1944–		Built in U.S.A., 1932–44.

Exhibition prepared for the U.S.O. by the Educational Program:

1943		Your Home—Your Design for Living.

Exhibitions prepared for the Office of War Information:

1943		The New Architecture in the United States.*
		For circulation in the Middle East. First showing, March 1944, in Cairo.
1944		U.S. Housing in War and Peace.*
		Exhibition directed by Mary Cooke, with Catherine Bauer as consultant. A special section on building techniques was prepared by the Standards Section of the National Housing Agency. For circulation in England.
1944		America Builds.*
		Modern American architecture and its immediate background, with a section on housing and a special section on regional and city planning organized by G. Holmes Perkins of the National Housing Agency. Assembled by Janet Henrich O'Connell. For circulation in Sweden.

Competition:

New Art Center for Wheaton College, conducted by the Department of Architecture and the *Architectural Forum.* 1938.

Films:

New Architecture at the London Zoo, prepared for the Museum and Harvard University by L. Moholy-Nagy. Shown and circulated with the exhibition, Modern Architecture in England. 1937.

Evolution of the Skyscraper, prepared with E. Francis Thompson, photographer. 1939.

Publications:

** published independently of any exhibition.

Built to Live in, by Philip Johnson. 1931.**

Modern Architecture. 1932. Essays on individual architects by Henry-Russell Hitchcock, Jr., and Philip Johnson; essay on housing by Lewis Mumford. Foreword by Alfred H. Barr, Jr. Also published as *Modern Architects* by the Museum of Modern Art and W. W. Norton & Co., New York, 1932.

Early Modern Architecture: Chicago, 1870–1910. 1933. Re-issued in 1940 because of popular demand. Mimeographed.

America Can't Have Housing? 1934. Edited by Carol Aronovici; this contains contributions from leaders in the field both here and in Europe.

Louis Sullivan, Prophet of Modern Architecture, by Hugh Morrison.** Published by the Museum of Modern Art and W. W. Norton & Co., New York, 1935.

The New Architecture and the Bauhaus, by Walter Gropius.** Published by the Museum of Modern Art and Faber & Faber Ltd., London, 1936.

The Architecture of H. H. Richardson and His Times, by Henry-Russell Hitchcock, Jr. 1936. The standard work on this great architect.

Modern Architecture in England. 1937. Essays by H.-R. Hitchcock, Jr., and Catherine Bauer; edited by Ernestine Fantl.

A New House by Frank Lloyd Wright on Bear Run, Pennsylvania. 1938.

Alvar Aalto: Architecture and Furniture. 1938. Essays by A. Lawrence Kocher and Simon Breines; foreword by John McAndrew.

Trois Siècles d'Art aux Etats-Unis. 1938. Essay on architecture in the United States by John McAndrew pp. 69–77.

The Bauhaus: 1919–1928. 1938. Edited by Herbert Bayer, Ise and Walter Gropius.

Art in Our Time. 1939. Essay on housing by Frederick A. Gutheim and John McAndrew, pp. 311–17. Catalog of the Tenth Anniversary Exhibition.

Guide to Modern Architecture in the Northeast States.** 1940. Edited with an introduction by John McAndrew. Foreword by Philip L. Goodwin.

What is Modern Architecture? 1942.

Brazil Builds: Architecture New and Old, 1652–1942, by Philip L. Goodwin. 1943.

GLOSSARY

articulation	Formulation of structure or plan in clearly distinguished and systematically interrelated parts
cantilever	A projecting beam or member fixed only at one end
clearstory	That part of a building which rises above roofs of other parts and which has windows in its walls
lally column	An exposed metal pipe-column, sometimes filled with concrete. Invented by Mr. Lally, a mason
lamination	The bonding together under pressure of thin layers to form an indissoluble whole
lintel	Horizontal member which spans a door or window opening
louvers	Adjustable or fixed window slats which exclude rain and sun but permit ventilation
plywood	Wood made up of an odd number of veneer sheets glued or otherwise bonded (not nailed) together, with the grain of each layer at right angles to that of adjacent layers
reinforced concrete	Concrete in which metal, usually steel rods, is embedded in such a manner that the two materials act together in resisting forces
sheathing	Flat boarding used to cover a structural wood frame
studs	The rectangular uprights of a light wooden frame; in typical American construction, studs are 2″ x 4″ and spaced 16″ from center to center
tongue-and-groove	A smooth joint between boards: one edge of each board has a projecting rib which fits into a corresponding groove on the edge of the next board
NHA	National Housing Agency
FPHA	Federal Public Housing Authority
FHA	Federal Housing Administration
FSA	Farm Security Administration

Five thousand seven hundred copies of the first edition of this book were printed in May, 1944, for the Trustees of The Museum of Modern Art by The Plantin Press, New York. Four thousand copies of the revised second edition were printed in October, 1944. Seven thousand copies of this third edition were printed in November, 1945.

Built in USA: Post-war Architecture